RESILIENCE UNLIMITED

How to Always Find Your Best Path

Chaplain (Major) Ret. Paul Lynn

WESTBOW
P R E S S®
A DIVISION OF THOMAS NELSON
& ZONDERVAN

WestBow Press books may be ordered through booksellers or by contacting:

WestBow Press
A Division of Thomas Nelson & Zondervan
1663 Liberty Drive
Bloomington, IN 47403
www.westbowpress.com
844-714-3454

Interior Image Credit: Zoe E. Elizabeth Lynn. The image
with Purpose Highway and Belonging Boulevard

ISBN: 979-8-3850-1314-2 (sc)
ISBN: 979-8-3850-1313-5 (e)

Library of Congress Control Number: 2023922506

Print information available on the last page.

WestBow Press rev. date: 02/21/2024

For my wife, Liz; my family; and chaplains.

Contents

Foreword

Chaplain (Major) Ret. Paul Lynn, in *Resilience Unlimited*, weaves together the fabric of human existence through what he has identified as the Seven Meaning Making Markers: meaning, purpose, belonging, values-based routines, spiritual intelligence, positive self-identity, and a horizon of hope. He has illuminated these facets of life, providing deep insights into the interconnectedness of our inner and outer worlds. When intentionally synthesized together the possibilities for resiliency are boundless.

At the heart of this project, he brings out the two main elements for resiliency: understanding one's spiritual identity and developing spiritual intelligence. In the broad scheme of the American marketplace, through familial ties and deep friendships, in the military communities of our joint forces, knowing who you are from the spiritual point of view is in need now more than ever. In the crucible of our times, statistically, our culture is losing this critical part of the self.

He addresses two of the great challenges of our Western world that are plaguing our culture: meaninglessness and character fragility. He cites relevant research that has brought this to the forefront. What Chaplain Lynn has done in *Resilience Unlimited* is create a resiliency tool to counteract these forces. The book allows you to reflect in real-time your own resilience needs, with what he calls a Pathfinder Resiliency Tool.

The outcome of proactive attention to these meaning making

markers on your Pathfinder Resiliency Tool is to find the best path to your ideal future-self, best path on your worst day, and best path for your every day. This is how he defines resilience. It's not just bouncing back, but finding your best path.

In this book, you are invited to explore the dimensions of these seven meaning making markers by answering the question, "Who am I?" This is what he calls the golden thread that runs throughout the book. As you navigate the complexities of this world we are continuously challenged with this question. The information here will equip you to answer it from your soul, the center of gravity, where resiliency is the strongest.

Harold G. Koenig, M.D., M.H.Sc.
Professor of Psychiatry and Behavioral Sciences
Associate Professor of Medicine
Duke University Medical Center, Durham, North Carolina
Adjunct Professor, Department of Medicine, King Abdulaziz University, Jeddah, Saudi Arabia
Visiting Professor, Shiraz University of Medical Sciences, Shiraz, Iran
Editor-in-Chief, *International Journal of Psychiatry in Medicine*

Preface

Welcome to *Resilience Unlimited: How to Always Find Your Best Path*! This isn't just a book; it's your guide to cultivating the most resilient mindset possible. Join me on a transformative journey as we navigate processes that culminate in a powerful one-page tool capturing the essence of resilience.

Crafted in the crucibles of active-duty military service and inspired from the soul of a US Army Chaplain, this handheld tool originated from humble yellow sticky notes used during Holistic Health and Fitness (H2F) Resiliency briefings at Fort Huachuca, Arizona. These short briefings were presented to Non-commissioned Officers (NCOs) during the dark hours of the winter mornings before the rigors of Physical Training (PT).

Multifaceted Origins

I want to express gratitude for the diverse influences that have intricately shaped this book. My wife's doctoral thesis on military moves and spiritual resilience, coupled with my PhD studies at the Institute of Lutheran Theology under the guidance of Dr. Dennis Bielfeldt, forms the bedrock of its theoretical foundation. The integration of my professional experiences and knowledge as a US Army Operational and Family Life Chaplain has given rise to a unified and comprehensive tool, providing intriguing insights that prove invaluable on your journey. Ultimately, this is a highly integrated tool that brings into focus a wealth of critical data, offering you perspectives that are both interesting and profoundly helpful.

Evolution from Pathfinder

Originally named as a program called, "Pathfinder: Finding Your Best Path on Your Worst Day," this material has evolved into *Resilience Unlimited*. While preserving the vocabulary of a pathfinder in resilience training, I introduce the Resilience Unlimited—Pathfinder Resiliency Tool (PRT). This isn't about earning a badge; it's about understanding your inherent neurological predisposition as a pathfinder, unlocking the key to consistently discovering your best path.

Acknowledgments and Development

I owe a debt of gratitude to the senior Chaplains in the Army who recognized the value of my early models. Their vision led me to profound worldwide beta-testing opportunities from 2021 to 2022. These presentations occurred through the US Army Chaplain Corps Spiritual Readiness Initiatives (SRI). Special thanks to Chaplain (Major General) Tom Solhjem, Retired, who created conditions for grassroots chaplain leadership, addressing complex problems like resiliency and suicide.

The material has transformed into a 2.0 product. The book is accompanied by an online Resilience Unlimited Assessment, a Field Manual, the Pathfinder Resiliency Tool—Meaning Map, a Certified Leader's Guide, PowerPoint slides, and training videos. I am thrilled about the formal training being offered by our new team, Trekk Unlimited, which you can explore further at www.trekkunlimited.com.

Purpose and Potential

Resilience Unlimited is more than a book; it's a mechanism for your future resiliency, guiding you toward your best path. It emphasizes the transformative effects achievable through its processes, providing insights that induce positive change. While it doesn't replace therapy, the book aims to help you build resilient conditions, minimizing the need for emergency external intervention. Remember, if you ever find yourself struggling to keep your head above water, both spiritually and psychologically, please don't hesitate to seek help. The national suicide prevention hotline number is 988.

Universal Applicability

The Resilience Unlimited model, born from science, psychology, philosophy, and theology, isn't weighted down by heavy theological discourse. Drawing from Christian theology and my personal relationship with God, it synthesizes ideas from many research giants. The universal principles of resilience outlined in the book are applicable to everyone, irrespective of religious or spiritual beliefs. (See Appendix 4 as an example).

Spiritual Identity and Diversity

Embarking on a journey through spirituality with a focus from Judeo-Christian thought, the book takes a non-prescriptive stance. However, from another religious standpoint, it invites a reflective exploration. Delve into your beliefs with a case study on identity discovered in Chapter 1. Whether you align with Christianity, embrace a non-religious stance, or follow another faith, the book unfolds valuable moral and psychological insights drawn from Biblical stories and many other multicultural and historical references.

It's essential to recognize that while the book provides a lens from mainly one religious viewpoint, it serves as a mirror, inviting readers from various traditions to reflect on how their own spiritual formation is shaped. Capturing the vast spectrum of spiritual identity and intelligence formations across all belief systems is an impossible feat, but this book hopes to be a catalyst for introspection and understanding. This model will accommodate all kinds of faith. A resiliency model like this has been sorely missing, until now. I hope you take it out for a significant test drive.

As we venture forward, join me in the exploration of self-discovery and resilience. May the Resilience Unlimited—Pathfinder Resiliency Tool be your unwavering companion as you navigate the challenges of life.

Introduction:
Why Resilience Unlimited?

Having a resilient mindset is essential equipment in the US Army. What did resiliency look like for me over the last three decades? The majority of time I spent in the Army was in airborne and special operations units. This meant parachuting out of high-performance aircraft, such as C-130s and C-17s, as well as Black Hawk and Chinook helicopters. The Army sent me into combat operations with deployments to Iraq and Afghanistan. I was awarded a Bronze Star from the 82nd Airborne Division. With an airborne unit in Alaska, we were deployed to a peacekeeping mission in Kosovo. In support of NATO forces to deter Russian aggression, I had the opportunity to serve as a Division Chaplain (Forward), visiting friendly forces across Eastern Europe.

Sometimes doing hard things took me past my personal and family limits. Just ask my wife of thirty years. I know what it feels like to fail and also be resilient by finding my best path forward. Building preventive resiliency, I learned how to deepen, develop, and diversify my personal and professional life conditions to prevent failure the next time. This was academically uncovered and experientially discovered.

I grew up as a pathfinder, a cross-country runner. Later, I was privileged to coach both struggling and winning collegiate cross-country teams. Running a sub-3:00 hour marathon is part of my personal history. I have run mountain, ultra-marathon distances in Alaska, Texas, and New Mexico. I have summited eight fourteen thousand feet peaks in Colorado. Recently, I scratched the Grand Canyon rim-to-rim-to-rim (R3) route, nearly forty-eight miles, off my running bucket list. It was a long, beautiful eighteen-hour day. I didn't run it alone though. I had two pathfinders with me. Two experienced ultrarunner off-duty border patrol agents who had run it previously were my sage guides. I employed the Resilience Unlimited principles found in this book to help me accomplish this bucket list goal. With them, it was a transformational day.

The Gold Thread

Some brief introductory comments about my background in resiliency are important, but I'm leading off with a special story about *why* this book should be important to you and what has motivated me to answer one of life's most troubling questions: how to be resilient on your worst day. The answer is found in this question: "Who am I?" This question is the gold thread that runs through the whole book.

It started on a beautiful Fourth of July morning. My wife, Liz, and I rose early to beat the heat of southern Arizona for a high-desert hike around the Huachuca mountain range. Because of its history and location, on the border of Mexico, those who are stationed there affectionately call it "the edge of the frontier." It's gorgeous.

The mountains are located in part of the Coronado National Forest. It's lined with hiking and mountain biking trails. There are hidden canyons with secret waterfalls. The community is called "the hummingbird capital of the world." Rising from the high desert floor are two main mountain peaks that reach over nine thousand feet. In the late spring, the city of Sierra Vista organizes a mountain race called the Sky Islands Challenge. The mountaintops overlooking the city are a place to behold.

That was what Liz and I wanted to get into that morning. It's a pathfinder's dream.

There was one liability to this plan. Over that holiday weekend, it was my turn to carry the on-call duty chaplain phone. I knew which area I wanted to hike. I wanted to explore a new trail, bag a small peak, and be available just in case I got a call.

Then it happened. Just as Liz and I were enjoying the sun and a vista, looking deep into Mexico, the duty phone rang. It was the casualty office. "Chaplain Lynn, I need you to come in and provide a notification to a family. You have a mission about an hour from here. It's a suicide."

That was a punch in the gut. I thought, *Wow, our country is celebrating Independence Day, the most important American holiday, with festivities and fireworks. I'm going to put on my dress blue uniform and deliver a horrible message to parents that their son killed himself last night.*

On a hot Arizona day, I consoled them in a time of tragedy. How many suicide notifications have I delivered to parents? One too many. The Christian philosopher Kierkegaard was right when he said that the greatest hazard in life is to lose yourself. Recent polling data says that 94% of all people believe suicides are preventable. I believe it, too. I don't just believe it; I have been motivated to do something about it by creating Resilience Unlimited, How to Always Find Your Best Path.

PART I

The Art and Science
of Resilience
Unlimited—Pathfinder
Resiliency Tool

I

Identity: Your Signature Question

Every day we wake up to the question "Who am I?" Therapist and theologian Henri Nouwen once preached a sermon titled "Life of the Beloved," saying, "This is the most important question in life."[1] The sermon reflects the title of his acclaimed book as well. However, in the book, he doesn't explicitly make this statement. As a trained trauma therapist and theologian myself, I attest he is absolutely correct.

Today more than ever, this question is thrust on us from a myriad of directions: the internet world, media, work, family, friends, politics, religion, and so on. We are not usually interrogated with an obvious frontal assault; more often, this question is felt implicitly. None of us can escape the fact that the question of identity is currently headline news. Answering this question in the best possible way leads us to an ideal future self. Failure to satisfactorily answer this question leads to anxiety and depression or even worse.

---

[1] Henry Nouwen, PhD, "Being the Beloved, Henry Nouwen (FULL SERMON PART 1) |Crystal Cathedral," Henry Nouwen Society, YouTube video, https://www.youtube.com/watch?v=trG7Oh_PopM&list=PLq385qyR7NY 6513dy9JAWZ7lvGCVgcQ2f. Henry Nouwen, a Catholic Priest, was born in the Netherlands and taught at Harvard, Yale, and Notre Dame.

The Resilience Unlimited
Thought Experiment

How do I know this is the most important question in life? When I provided this resiliency training to soldiers, I would pose this thought-experiment question: Imagine you are selected to participate in a game show like *Survivor*. You have the opportunity to win millions of dollars and gain notoriety. You fly out to a remote island in the Pacific. When the plane takes off again, you realize you are all alone. No one else is there. You understand it's physically impossible to leave. However, there is enough food on the island to survive for the rest of your life. My question to you now is, "Who are you?" Pause for a second and let that question set in. How will you answer that question?

On multiple iterations of this training, some soldiers would verbalize ideas of resiliency, others authentic suicidal ideations! The latter would sound something like this: "I would kill myself in that situation." Then another soldier would say, "I was thinking the same thing!" In that thought experiment, I stripped away their present purpose in life, significant belonging relationships, and values-based routines that gave them meaning in life. Oftentimes, at the conclusion of the training, soldiers would reflect and share to me how they were thinking about the Tom Hanks movie *Cast Away*. They could relate to how Tom Hanks's character emotionally fell apart while desperately trying to survive after losing his volleyball and friend, which he named Wilson.

US Army soldiers are a microcosm of the larger macrocosm of American culture. Today more than ever, young people are struggling to find a developed sense of self and resiliency. They are trying to figure out their identity: "who am I?" New York University psychologist Dr. Johnathan Haidt has accurately chronicled this problem, labeling it a "national crisis." It is a problem he has identified as character fragility.[2] This is one of the unanswered problems of identity.

Now let's move from an imagined deserted island to a historically real Nazi prison where identity was wrestled to the ground. German pastor and theologian Dietrich Bonhoeffer was captured by the Nazi government for sedition. He was a member of a small resistance group that conspired to assassinate Adolf Hitler. In this poem that he wrote while in prison before his death, he reflected on the same internal experience, having his identity threatened and stripped away. However, it concluded with a determinative statement of resilience based on his identity. It was called "Who Am I?"

Who am I? They often tell me
I stepped from my cell's confinement
Calmly, cheerfully, firmly,
Like a squire from his country-house.
Who am I? They often tell me
I used to speak to my warders
Freely and friendly and clearly,
As though it were mine to command.
Who am I? They also tell me
I bore the days of misfortune
Equably, smilingly, proudly,
Like one accustomed to win.

Am I then really all that which other men tell of?
Or am I only what I myself know of myself?
Restless and longing and sick, like a bird in a cage,

---

[2] Jonathan Haidt, PhD, https://jonathanhaidt.com/. Dr. Haidt has tremendous resources documenting fragility.

Struggling for breath, as though hands were compressing my throat,
Yearning for colours, for flowers, for the voices of birds,
Thirsting for words of kindness, for neighbourliness,
Tossing in expectation of great events,
Powerlessly trembling for friends at infinite distance,
Weary and empty at praying, at thinking, at making,
Faint, and ready to say farewell to it all?
Who am I? This or the other?
Am I one person today and tomorrow another?
Am I both at once? A hypocrite before others,
And before myself a contemptibly woebegone weakling?
Or is something within me still like a beaten army,
Fleeing in disorder from victory already achieved?

Who am I? They mock me, these lonely questions of mine.
Whoever I am, thou knowest, O God, I am Thine![3]

Bonhoeffer rightly struggled with his identity. His purpose, belonging, and values-based routines were stripped down. But his core identity remained intact. He knew who he was. He was God's beloved son. This is where one's ultimate sense of resiliency is located.

---

[3] Dietrich Bonhoeffer, *Letters and Papers from Prison*, ed. Eberhard Bethge, trans. Reginald H. Fuller (New York: Macmillan Company, 1953), 221–22.

A Case Study: Christian Identity is Received, Not Achieved

In my estimation, no modern theologian summarizes the critical importance of understanding core identity better than Pastor Tim Keller. In numerous Gospel Coalition resources, he can be found saying this: "Your identity is received, not achieved."[4] What does he mean by this?

He remarks that Christianity is the only religion in which you do not decide your identity. It is received. "But to all who did receive him, who believed in his name, he gave the right to become children of God, who were born, not of blood nor of the will of the flesh nor of the will of man, but of God" (John 1:12–13). Christian identity is internally received by faith and externally through initiation of water baptism (John 3:5).

Christian spiritual formation through water baptism validates the faith experience. This is why theologian Martin Luther is known to have said, "Remember your baptism!" Can people baptize themselves? No, that's ridiculous. It must be given *to you* by someone else, namely, a *bona fide* representative of the church. Christian identity is not performed or achieved. It is received.

When I was a kid, the first time I ever stepped into the ocean, I got caught in a riptide. I had no idea what it was. I was drowning and about to die. Instead, I called out for help to the lifeguard. He was a hulking athlete who swam out with a life preserver. He rescued me from near death. This is what Peter means when he says, "Baptism saves you" (1 Peter 3:21). Identity is received, not achieved. You can't do it. It is done for you.

When you compare an identity that is achieved with an identity that is received, you can see a stark difference. When

---

[4] Tim Keller, "What Is Your Identity?," Gospel Coalition, April 2019, YouTube video, https://www.youtube.com/watch?v=A1jHQE3YmPU. Dr. Tim Keller is an author of 31 books.

I was a collegiate cross-country runner, it was a motivational tradition for our team to gather at our coach's house before the last race of the season to eat pasta and watch the movie *Chariots of Fire*. The movie reveals the contrast of these two identities. The story is a historical dramatization of two British Olympic track athletes who qualify for the Paris Olympics in 1924. In the movie, Harold Abrams is a non-observant, ethnic Jewish athlete about to run the one-hundred-yard dash. He famously tells his coach, "I have ten seconds to justify my existence." In comparison, the Christian athlete, Eric Liddell, lives by the mantra "When I run, I feel God's pleasure." When both of those athletes toe the line in Paris, are both of them nervous? Yes. However, you can see the difference between anxiety in the self and assurance from God.

The Voice of God as Identity

The theological centerpiece for identity is received by the voice of God telling us, "You are the beloved." It is clear in the biblical story where Christ entered the Jordan River to be baptized. The heavens were opened, and the Spirit of God descended like a dove. A voice from heaven said, "This is my beloved Son, with whom I am well pleased" (Matthew 3:16–17).

What happened next? In Mark's gospel, the story revealed that the Holy Spirit drove Jesus into the desert to fast, where he was tempted by the devil for forty days. It is important to understand the three temptation events as an attack on Christ's identity. There is a significant connection between the baptismal voice of God and Satan's strategy to denounce it.

The three temptations are universal in scope for us as well:

1. Will we try to complete our identity with our own power (Luke 4:3–4)?

2. Will we live for the viral voice of popularity instead of God's by doing something spectacular (Matthew 4:5–6)?
3. Will we associate our identity with the things that we can possess (Matthew 4:8–9)?

In other words, will we rely on what we do, what others say, and what we have? There are multiple variations of these questions about our identity that are posed to us daily. The questions attempt to dislodge the importance of our spiritual identity with other competing external realities. These questions attempt to move the boundary of our spiritual identity where we feel ultimate confidence and hope.

For Christ, under these temptations, his mission was to pass the test as the second Adam. The first Adam, created in the image of God, failed his God-given identity in the garden. The second Adam, Christ, the image of the invisible God (Colossians 1:15), who is both God and man, was the only one who could pass the test. This was accomplished through reliance on his God-given identity.

Christ, in his ministry, relied on his relationship identity within the Godhead to sustain himself. This was how he was resilient. Christ's identity was tested in the desert and retested again and again. Peter tried to persuade him to stop talking about his impending death on the cross. Jesus rebuked Peter, saying, "Get behind me, Satan! For you are not setting your mind on the things of God, but on the things of man" (Mark 8:33).

Afterward, Christ's identity was revalidated on the mount of transfiguration (Matthew 17:5) as he began to point toward his final days in Jerusalem, moving toward the passion. He needed this revalidating voice to remain resilient as he moved into the final days of suffering. His identity never stopped being tested, even while hanging on the cross. He was pressured to relinquish his identity (Matthew 27:40). He was taunted that if he was the Son of God, he should save himself.

From a psychological perspective, Christ on the cross calls out to God by quoting Psalm 22:1: "My God, my God, why have you forsaken me?" These are words expressing emotional abandonment, a psychological gap between himself and the Father. But at a much deeper and profound theological state, the final thoughts of Psalm 22:30-31 anchors his identity in promise and hope. "Posterity shall serve him; it shall be told of the Lord to the coming generation; they shall come and proclaim his righteousness to a people yet unborn that he has done it." John, his disciple standing there witnessing his death, records Jesus's last words: "It is finished" (John 19:30). Christ accomplished this ultra-human feat through his identity.

Our resiliency is being tested every day by the question "Who am I?" Recently, my wife was diagnosed with cancer. Before her surgery, I couldn't help projecting my life into the future. "Who am I without her? What will my life look like?" There were dark feelings associated with this. When our identity is being questioned, or even threatened, like this, it cuts deep. Being a husband to my wife of thirty years is a significant part of my identity.

What does your life look like if you lose your job or a relationship or if you move across the country? Transitions wreck identity, especially when they occur without your permission. This is why it's so important to know who you are spiritually. Spiritual identity is the center of gravity for lifelong resiliency. Gen. George C. Marshall is regularly quoted in the US Army Chaplain Corps as saying, "The Soldier's heart, the Soldier's spirit, the Soldier's soul, are everything. Unless the Soldier's soul sustains him, he cannot be relied on and will fail himself and his commander and his country in the end." It is the realization of your spiritual identity, found in the voice of God that matters most.

2

Supercharged Resiliency:
Always Finding Your Best Path

Every day you are posed with the question "Who am I?" Knowing who you are spiritually, being confident in your role identity, and deftly handling your psychological identity are fundamental to having a supercharged resilient life. The first key to resiliency is to know who you are spiritually. Once you are set in your core identity, which is spiritual identity, you are ready to find your best path. This is your inner God-given identity.

Second, there are many other ways we understand ourselves. In the Resilience Unlimited—Pathfinder Resiliency Tool, these are role identities. I am a husband and a father. I consider myself a runner, a much slower one now since I'm in my fifties, but this is what I have done for self-care and enjoyment all my life. I have been an Army Chaplain, and I still function that way. All these roles are exterior identities and can change without our permission. Daily, ensuring clear boundaries to our role identities with the right perspective and energy provide us confidence and hope. The Pathfinder Resiliency Tool can help you stay in touch with maintaining and developing healthy boundaries.

Third, we have psychological identities. These identities are how we see ourselves. This can also be called an inner identity or a meta identity. It is the narratives we believe. Oftentimes, this inner psychological identity has been developed from what people have said about us in the past. We develop a psychological identity in how we see ourselves in the future. This meta identity oftentimes gravitates around performance, failure, and achievement. Psychological identity is highly influenced by social factors. The Pathfinder Resiliency Tool can help you manage the various narratives about ourselves that we often think about.

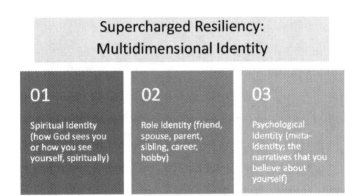

Figure 1

Here is the challenge when it comes to resiliency. In our everyday life, sometimes we do not feel like our exterior identity and our interior identity line up well. In a psychological sense, I might say, "I am not a good father or husband," "I am not lovable," "I am not smart," or "I am a poor performer." There is an infinite amount of negative self-narratives that we can label ourselves within the psychological identity.

Sometimes people underestimate themselves and relate to the idea of imposter syndrome. On the other hand, we can overestimate our psychological identity too. That could be narcissistic. The apostle Paul, in Romans 12:3, says, "For by the grace given to me I say to everyone among you not to think of himself more highly than he ought to think, but to think with sober judgment, each according to the measure of faith that God has assigned." The bottom line here is to not think lower or higher about ourselves but with sober judgment.

It's important to pay attention to the overcritical and rosy narratives we listen to about ourselves in our psychological identity. This psychological identity is often making appraisals of your self. The Pathfinder Resiliency Tool can help you bring this into a healthy perspective. It does this by empowering your spiritual identity, through your spiritual intelligence, to put the psychological identity in its proper place.

To reiterate, when it comes to resiliency, it is your spiritual identity, in knowing that God loves you no matter what, that can enable you to withstand the loss of an exterior identity or a challenge to an inner psychological identity. The spiritual identity through your faith provides an infinite connection and resource to becoming resilient in life.

Definition of *Resiliency*

I have used the word *resiliency* many times so far. The most common definitional understanding of *resiliency* is "to bounce back." Communicating resiliency as bouncing back speaks about effect. This is helpful, but there is a better way of understanding it.

Life is changing every day. It's dynamic, not static. We are constantly being challenged with the question "Who am I?" in our spiritual identity, role identity, and psychological identity. No one is ever bouncing back to the same time-driven homeostasis. Our life is always in draft. I'm older today than I was yesterday. The boundaries of our exterior and interior identities are always being tested—if not now, wait a minute. We are always moving into a new normal. That is why it is important to define *resiliency* as "finding your best path." Understanding the critical multidimensions of resiliency (spiritual, role, and psychological) is essential to having a supercharged resiliency.

This book is going to give you a tool for life so that you always find your best path. If you have a best path to your ideal future self and a best path on your worst day, then you will have a best path for your every day. This is developed in your Pathfinder Resiliency Tool.

Comprehensive Resiliency

Suicide has been at epidemic proportions and on the rise since pre-COVID-19. Many complex factors have exacerbated our national social fabric. Job dissatisfaction (purpose in life) and loneliness (belonging in life) are two of the top three social maladies of the world, right behind world hunger, as Gallup reports in 2023. The psychologist at the University of Toronto, Dr. John Vervaeke describes our time as "The Meaning Crisis."[5] This is the other unanswered question to identity.

What is a significant example of this? In September of 2023, the Guardian newspaper reported, "Doctors are dying by suicide at higher rates than the general population. Somewhere between 300 to 400 physicians a year in the US take their own lives, the equivalent of one medical school graduating annually."[6] This is just one strong indicator among many.

Originally, I developed Resilience Unlimited as a preventive tool to stop the epidemic of suicide in the US Army and for soldiers to become the most resilient as possible to the rigors of

---

[5] John Vervaeke, PhD, "Awakening from the Meaning Crisis, A 50-part Lecture Series," https://johnvervaeke.com/series/awakening-from-the-meaning-crisis/; Dr. Vervaeke has a book coming out by this title in 2024.
[6] Christiana Frangou, "US Surgeons are Killing Themselves at Alarming Rate," *The Guardian*, September, 2023.

military life. However, the tool is universally applicable. The Pathfinder Resiliency Tool is available to answer these two social maladies: character fragility and meaninglessness.

What does Resilience Unlimited do for you that's different from any other self-help program, counseling method, coaching model, or resiliency training? It provides (1) individual resiliency, (2) conditions-based resiliency, (3) and a unified-focused resiliency, and (4) it's holistic, integrated, and designed to provide maximum preventive resiliency against catastrophic meaning loss. The Pathfinder Resiliency Tool is designed to help provide you with a mechanism to reverse engineer and prohibit the permanent effects of catastrophic meaning loss.

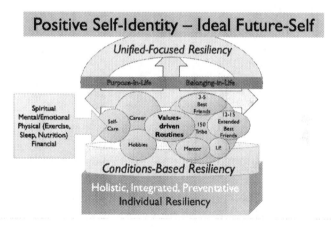

Figure 2

There's a lot to unpack in what I have just said in the above paragraph and in viewing this model. As you read on, you will see how this all fits together. As far as I know, no one brings this together for a comprehensive effect like this. You might think, *Do I really need this?* My experience working with elite special operations forces makes me say yes!

On one Christmas Eve while in Bagram, Afghanistan, my

Special Ops Commander dispatched me to a compound where the commander of Navy SEALs took his life. Everyone is a potential candidate for catastrophic meaning loss. Everyone can benefit from this. Like Noah and the ark, it's important to build it before you meet tragedy.

Here is what you will take away from Resilience Unlimited. By reading and following the Pathfinder Resiliency Tool model you will have (1) a plan to find the best path toward your ideal future-self, (2) a plan to find your best path on your worst day, and (3) a plan to find your best path for your every day. If you have a plan to find your ideal future self on the high end of life and a plan to be resilient on the low end of your worst day of life, then you can have a baseline plan for your every day of life.

How do I know you can do this? You are *already* a pathfinder. There is a science behind this statement. I want to help you find your art.

Always Running Ahead

Throughout the book, I'm going to be citing relatively new evidence-based neuroscience models of psychology validating philosophical principles, professional reflections, and biblical narratives that have stood the test of time. Out of this synthesis comes the Pathfinder Resiliency Tool. When you read it, the value of the Resilience Unlimited model will become immediately self-evident to you.

A white paper I wrote for the US Army Chief of Chaplains started out like this: "Facts. Human beings are already pathfinders. Neuroscientists describe the brain as a 'prediction machine.'"[7] David J. Linden, PhD, professor of neuroscience at Johns Hopkins University, describes this process in an article

---

[7] Benjamin Hardy, PhD, *Be Your Future Self Now* (Carlsbad, CA: Hay House, Inc., 2022), xxv.

in the *Atlantic*.[8] He says, "Rather than merely reacting to the external world the brain spends much of its time and energy actively making predictions about the future ... They can't be turned off through mere force of will. And because our brains are organized to predict the near future, it presupposes that there will, in fact, be a near future."

You are always orienting yourself to what comes next. The twentieth-century German philosopher Martin Heidegger called this *vorlaufen*. This means "always running ahead." Human beings are always running ahead to predict what can happen in the future. We are looking ahead toward the next end state of what we desire. This can mean thinking about having a sandwich for lunch, what college to attend, where you want to retire, or who you want beside you when you die. In essence, we are already pathfinders because we are curious, desirous, investigative, and protective beings. This runs inside us automatically. Philosopher James K. A. Smith says it this way:

> [W]hat makes us who we are, the kind of people we are—is what we love. More specifically, our identity is shaped by what we ultimately love or what we love as ultimate— what, at the end of the day, gives us a sense of meaning, purpose, understanding, and orientation to our being-in-the world. What we desire or love ultimately is a (largely implicit) vision of what we hope for, what we think the good life looks like. This vision of the good life shapes all kinds of actions and

---

[8] David J. Linden, "A Neuroscientist Prepares for Death, Lessons My Terminal Cancer Has Taught Me about the Mind," *Atlantic*, December 2021.

decisions and habits that we undertake, often without our thinking about it.[9]

There is a unique internal template inside each of us that drives us to our future. Having your spiritual core received first is the most important. Then you are fully equipped with the essential capability to find the path to your realistic goals. You can have a clearer vision for what you want your life to look like. What you love or desire spiritually shapes the future to your ideal future self. The problem is when you get stuck. This is where the Pathfinder Resiliency Tool provides the framework to help you solve the problem and be resilient.

[9] James K. A. Smith, *Desiring the Kingdom, Worship, Worldview and Cultural Formation*, vol. 1 of *Cultural Liturgies* (Grand Rapids, MI: Baker Academic, 2009), 26–27.

3

The Seven Meaning-Making Markers

I f you find yourself in agreement with scientists, philosophers, or theologians that we are always running ahead, the question you should ask is, "Why?" Why are we always running ahead? It is because we can't stop searching for meaning in life. Our meaning in life comes from the three pillars and is informed by the level of our spiritual intelligence.

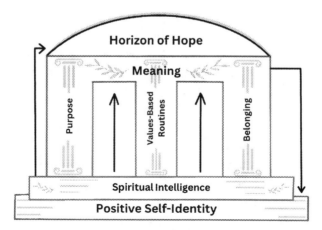

Figure 3

This figure is what I call the Seven Meaning-Making Markers model. I will help you synthesize these seven essential parts as they already exist in you. I am just helping you intracoordinate them. You do this in real time. Therefore, it's a synthesis and synchronization, so you can maximize your personal resiliency. You are always running ahead to ensure that you have the meaning that you desire.

Viktor Frankl, a well-known twentieth-century Jewish psychologist and Nazi concentration camp survivor, said something like this: "We need meaning in life like we need oxygen." [10] This is the aphoristic summary from his groundbreaking book *Man's Search for Meaning*. It can be said that meaning is the primary motivational force of humankind. Dr. Frankl observed that when prisoners in the concentration camp lost their meaning in life, they lost their will to live. They reached catastrophic meaning loss. When you lose your meaning in life, it's possible your identity begins to disintegrate.

Meaning Gives You Identity and Hope

In 2008, I was reassigned to the 82nd Airborne Division so I could deploy to Iraq with paratrooper infantrymen. I became the Battalion Chaplain for the 2nd of the 505th Parachute Infantry Regiment. I wanted to serve among these brave modern American warriors.

I went to Airborne School at Fort Benning (now Fort Moore), Georgia. I couldn't be a paratrooper chaplain without airborne wings, the distinguishing mark of paratrooper identity. I was already a part of a staff of over half a dozen other captains who were operationalizing the future mission. However, I was still unofficially initiated.

---

[10] Viktor Frankl, *Man's Search for Meaning* (Boston, MA: Beacon Press, 1992).

My Battalion Commander was going to test my mettle before he took me into a yearlong combat deployment to Southeast Baghdad, Iraq. He previously served in the US Army Rangers. He was the ultimate ranger: He was an extremely savvy and aggressive leader. He was incredibly strong and could run like the wind. He had perfectly manicured blond hair, piercing blue eyes, and a chiseled square jaw. He tested me like no other.

Two-Panther, as the unit was nicknamed, just finished a fifteen-month bloody deployment to Iraq and was full of experienced paratroopers. I wondered, "Do I have what it takes?" to be a paratrooper Chaplain in combat. Before the deployment, there was one day the Commander physically, mentally, and spiritually tested me more than ever.

At 0615, my fellow staff officers and I lined up in formation. We stood at attention and waited for reveille to play, with canons shooting off in the distance. In our physical training (PT) uniforms on a humid summer day, we saluted the flag in unison with crisp robotic arm movements. He then called us to do a right face, and he started to run us—hard.

He never told us where we were going. We just followed him into uncertainty as fast as we could. He kept a near-seven-minute-mile pace for the first mile until we climbed an exceptionally long hill. We hung on as he surged to the top. As soon as everyone gathered together, he ordered us to start doing crunches, with our backs hanging into the street. He didn't quit until we were nearing muscle failure.

He then commanded us to get up and keep running. We were now on the famous road called Ardennes. With his speed, he was dropping the hammer with a gliding pace. There were two majors who were falling behind. I started getting nervous but was keeping up. Then it happened.

I thought I heard a command to run to the front of the pack. So I sprinted past the commander, who was on the left side. His head shifted quickly to look at me and said, "Chaplain! What are you doing?" He commanded me to go to the sidewalk, do fifty flutter kicks, and then catch up to the formation while the rest of the officers kept running down Ardennes. When I caught up, he commanded me to do this twice more, until we saw a dog.

A stray dog was running down the street with a brown paper bag in its mouth. He commanded me to catch the dog! It easily outran me. The commander and staff officers kept running. He then called out for me to return to the group. When I caught up, he said in a flat, unemotional tone, "Chaplain, what did you learn this morning?"

I said, "Sir, never pass you again."

He said, "That's right, Chaplain. Never do that again."

We made it back to the battalion area, and he ordered us to circle up. He told us we were going to fight one another. At this point, I was already exhausted mentally and physically. I began to pray, "God, am I going to be accepted in this unit?" I started to question if I could pass this unofficial initiation. Who would I be if I failed?

Most of my fellow staff officers looked like they could be on the cover of muscle magazines. He began to call us out two at a time to square off using jujitsu, lunging, taking each other down, pinning our opponent in the dirt. The odds of me pinning those gorillas were impossibly small. They crushed me.

It was 0830 when he finally ended our PT test. I belonged for now. I could withstand punishing, humiliating physical training that could set me up for a combat fight.

My special operations Command Sergeant Major would regularly say, "Every day is selection." Yesterday is not good enough. You are competing on the job to be selected for today, every day. Your past does not matter. Winning means what you can do right now.

What sustained me in these rigorous training and combat environments? My spiritual identity. I believed. This is what ultimately gives us hope. In the Integrated Model of Resiliency, I give a breakdown analysis of this experience.

An Integrated Model of Resiliency

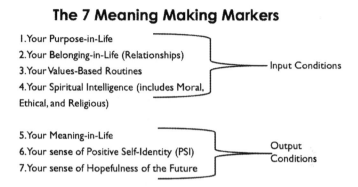

The 7 Meaning Making Markers

1. Your Purpose-in-Life
2. Your Belonging-in-Life (Relationships)
3. Your Values-Based Routines ⎫ Input Conditions
4. Your Spiritual Intelligence (includes Moral, Ethical, and Religious)

5. Your Meaning-in-Life
6. Your sense of Positive Self-Identity (PSI) ⎫ Output Conditions
7. Your sense of Hopefulness of the Future

Figure 4

The Pathfinder Resiliency Tool is an integration of many different sources of research. My wife's doctoral thesis is called "Finding Meaning in a Move: A Faith-Based Approach to a Permanent Change of Station (PCS)." I am a trained and experienced US Army Family Life Chaplain with a Master of Divinity and a Master's in Marriage and Family Therapy. I have a specialization in trauma therapy. I've been working on a PhD in Philosophical Theology.

One important source of resiliency-focused content emerged from the *US Army Field Manual FM 7-22*, paragraph 10, on the topic of spiritual resiliency. It reads,

> 10-2. Spirituality is often described as a sense of connection that gives meaning and purpose to a person's life. It is unique to each individual. The spiritual dimension applies to all people, whether religious and non-religious.
>
> Identifying one's purpose, core values, beliefs, identity, and life vision defines the

spiritual dimension. These elements, which define the essence of a person, enable one to build inner strength, make meaning of experiences, behave ethically, persevere through challenges, and be resilient when faced with adversity. An individual's spirituality draws upon parts of personal, philosophical, psychological, and religious teachings or beliefs, and forms the basis of their character.

This definition of resiliency from the US Army is also mirrored in both the Navy and Air Force official publications. Essentially, you can see some of the meaning-making markers in this definition of what makes up spiritual resilience. When you look at the Seven Meaning-Making Markers, all of them were on trial in my real-life scenario. My purpose in life was at stake as a chaplain. Could I be a paratrooper chaplain? My belonging (sense of connection) with others was on the line. Would I be accepted by the commander and staff? Physical training was an essential values-based routine. Could I physically do it? Failure in this was not an option.

It is these three that give meaning in life: purpose, belonging, values-based routines. It is the direct meaning from these factors that gives you a sense of positive self-identity. The courage and grit that sustained me was derived from my personal belief in God, that the Lord wanted me to serve paratroopers. With these markers present, I then had a horizon of hope.

The Resilience Unlimited Thread

If you know who you are spiritually, you can be resilient toward anything. I offer you a twenty-first-century solution as a protective factor against (1) fragility (2) and meaninglessness.

The Pathfinder Resiliency Tool captures these important Seven Meaning-Making Markers required for you to have resiliency. This is the beginning of understanding what it means to have holistic, integrated, and preventive resiliency.

> The thread that will run through this book is this: If you have a deepened, developed, and diversified purpose, belonging, and values-based routines, informed and guided by your spiritual intelligence (clarified moral, ethical, and spiritual values and virtues), you will have a more robust meaning in life. This gives you a positive self-identity (PSI) as opposed to a negative self-identity (NSI). A negative self-identity has scripts of defeat running through one's mind, such as existential angst about the future. An NSI becomes present when there is a significant lack in meaning-making markers.

Take, for example, the biblical story of Naomi in the book of Ruth. Naomi lost not only her husband but also her two sons. This was her whole significant biological belonging network. After those deaths, she returned home, and her NSI sounded like this: "Do not call me, Naomi; call me Mara, for the Almighty has dealt very bitterly with me" (Ruth 1:20). She took on a bitter identity. This lasted until the conditions of her family changed. She then took on a positive self-identity as "redeemed" with an aura of "blessing" to the Lord (Ruth 4:14).

When you have a present PSI and your conditions are robust, you can look out into the future as a horizon of hope and more adequately deal with the difficulties and complexities of life. I will continue to show you why and how this works.

4

From Meaning Gap to Meaning Map

Meaning Map to Close the Meaning Gap

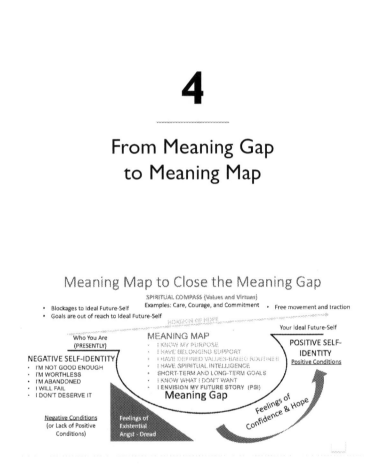

Figure 5

Fyodor Dostoevsky, a Russian novelist and author of *Crime and Punishment*, is known to have penned, "The mystery of existence lies not in just staying alive, but in finding something to live for." I want you to notice the little word *for*. It points to something or someone. Meaning is the result of purpose, belonging, and values-based routines—pointing *toward* something, heading *for* something. In Greek, the word *telos* means "end" or end state. This is very important when understanding meaning in the Pathfinder Resiliency Tool.

Philosopher James K. A. Smith explains it this way: "The place we unconsciously strive toward is what ancient philosophers of habit called our *telos*—our goal, our end. But the *telos* we live toward is not something we primarily know or believe or think about; rather, our *telos* is what we want, what we long for, what we crave. It is less an ideal that we have ideas about and more of a vision of 'the good life' that we desire."[11] This quote is pure gold because Smith shows the phenomena that drives us to what we want using philosophical language and accurately describes our behavior. What happens when we can't achieve this?

Another day when I was the on-call duty chaplain, I received a very serious call from a soldier. He said that if I didn't meet him within the next five minutes, he was going to kill himself. I asked him an obvious question. "When you look out into your horizon, what do you see?" He said, "I can't see past the next five minutes." This is the meaning gap in figure 5. He had a blockage that was preventing hope and was seriously depressed. Sometimes the goal on the horizon, the desired future self, is so far way it seems unreachable. It then feels like separation anxiety and promotes depression.

The Pathfinder Resiliency Tool helps you cross the meaning gap with a planned meaning map. The PRT Meaning Map does help you define what your vision of the good life can be. However, the PRT is less about the question "What is the good life you desire?" and more about the vision of "What is your ideal future self?" There are evidenced-based reasons why I provide this important shift of questioning that will be very helpful for you. The quality of your subjective sense of meaning in life is found in this shift.

---

[11] James K. A. Smith, *You Are What You Love: The Spiritual Power of Habit* (Grand Rapids, MI: Brazos Press, 2016), 11.

The Gap

All of us at any given moment have a meaning gap. In between who you are and who you want to be is a gap. If I ask you, "What does your future look like?" you immediately begin to project what it can be. But you are not there yet. It takes something to get you there—a plan. And in between the gap, without a plan, is existential angst and perhaps sadness or depression. Negative narratives about yourself begin to run through your mind that most likely are not true. Doubts and negative scripts start to emerge.

This is what we experience when we are faced with a meaning gap. All of us have an ideal future self in mind. All of us have an innate desire to run ahead to potential possibilities. The gap calls us to question, "Who am I really?" The gap becomes a boundary that has the potential to erode the confidence of our spiritual, role, or psychological identity.

Resiliency is finding your best path to your ideal future self. You are being the most resilient when you are moving proactively toward the person you want to become. You are deepening, developing, and diversifying yourself in the conditions of your life (see figure 2). If you are intentionally growing stronger in your conditions, you will be healthier and happier and live longer, reaching your goals toward your ideal future self. The science behind living with purpose in your life—have three to five best friends to share it, develop values-based routines to keep yourself physically fit, practice your religion, and much more—strengthens the conditions of your life; all help you be resilient.

If your conditions in life are thin, fragile, or few, you are less likely to be resilient. Think of having only one egg in one basket. If that egg breaks, you now have nothing. However, if you have multiple baskets with multiple eggs, you have the ability to withstand threats and losses.

Let me give you another example. Someone put in an application for a new job in which he was highly qualified. He was desperate for a career change and improvement in salary. His dream job was on the West Coast. He was on the East. He received several phone and Zoom interviews. He was then flown out to meet important stakeholders in the company over several days and still received no decision. He moved to the West Coast anyway. After he settled in, he received a call for another interview for the job. At the last minute, he was waived off by a text message. Someone else was now a candidate. He had one egg in one basket. He didn't have any other applications or résumés anywhere else. He was anxious and depressed. He felt as if he couldn't reach his ideal future self.

However, he was qualified for many other jobs. He began to send résumés to other companies and different places. He quit having tunnel vision and changed his conditions from a potential single point of failure to the possibilities of multiple positions. He now felt more confident and less anxious. There could be another source of income. He expanded his conditions with additional resources.

Meaning gaps tend to send us into an NSI that is not true. To close the gap, I created the Pathfinder Resiliency Tool Meaning Map. It helps you develop comprehensive resiliency. In business or military leadership, sometimes it's called an individual development plan (IDP). The Pathfinder Resiliency Tool is more than an IDP; it's a tool that grows with your life.

Figure 6. The Pathfinder Resiliency Tool Meaning Map

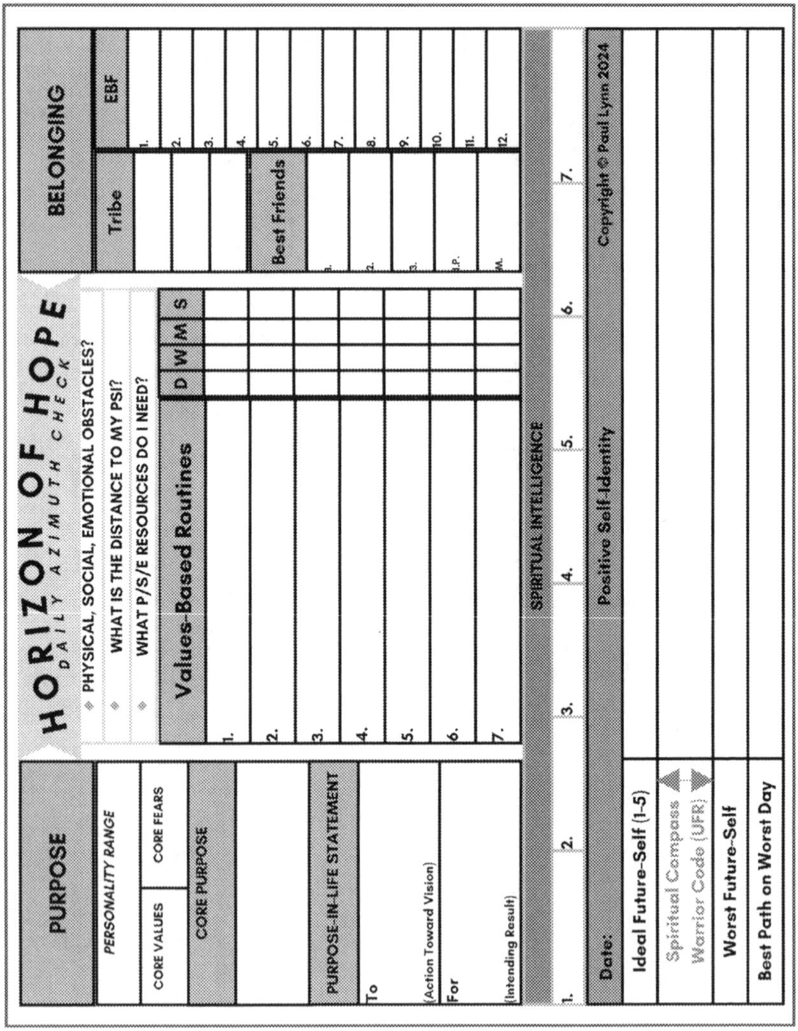

HORIZON OF HOPE
DAILY AZIMUTH CHECK

- PHYSICAL, SOCIAL, EMOTIONAL OBSTACLES?
- WHAT IS THE DISTANCE TO MY PSI?
- WHAT P/S/E RESOURCES DO I NEED?

PURPOSE

PERSONALITY RANGE

CORE VALUES	CORE FEARS

CORE PURPOSE

PURPOSE-IN-LIFE STATEMENT

To

[Action Toward Vision]

For

[Intending Result]

Values-Based Routines

	D	W	M	S
1.				
2.				
3.				
4.				
5.				
6.				
7.				

BELONGING

Tribe	EBF
	1.
	2.
	3.
	4.
	5.
	6.
	7.
	8.
	9.
	10.
	11.
	12.

Best Friends
1.
2.
3.
J.P.
M.

Copyright © Paul Lynn 2024

SPIRITUAL INTELLIGENCE

1. 2. 3. 4. 5. 6. 7.

Positive Self-Identity

Date:

Ideal Future-Self (1-5)

Spiritual Compass
Warrior Code (UFR)

Worst Future-Self

Best Path on Worst Day

In Part II of this book, you will be trained how to fill out your Pathfinder Resiliency Tool. This is a step-by-step, easy process. At first glance, some of this is very intuitive. It's not complex. Don't let it intimidate you. This resiliency tool can help you reflectively mediate the conditions to your ideal future self and best path on your worst day and give you a standard to successfully live your best path for your every day. For downloadable copies of the Resilience Unlimited—Pathfinder Resiliency Tool go to: www.trekkunlimited.com.

Definition of *Meaning* in the Map

What is meaning? Academics have written volumes on this topic. As a resilient pathfinder, the understanding of meaning is the subjective sense that something or someone is significant and valuable to you. Meaning involves faith and confidence in the positive conditions of relationships, activities, beliefs, institutions, and structures. As already said, there is a desired search for its presence.

Meaning is associated with joy. It's different from happiness. There is a sense of satisfaction with meaning. Happiness is known as feeling pleasure. It's important to differentiate these two. Both can be meaningful. Researchers conclude that meaning can have a greater effect on our well-being than happiness. We need meaning in life like we need oxygen.

Your meaning in life is your religion. *Religio*, the Latin word for *religion*, means "to bind." Your primary meaning in life is what binds your life together. Now look at the Pathfinder Resiliency Tool Meaning Map (figure 6). These are the important elements that you will write out and bind your life together.

Everyone has a religion, whether you believe in a transcendent higher power or God or use transcendental practices to help you cope with life. Perhaps you use both. We all have a certain amount of faith in medicine, machines, and government. It's impossible not to have faith. If you fly across the country, you have faith that the jet is being coordinated by competent pilots and air traffic controllers and sustained by mechanics. You ultimately don't know, but you have faith and trust that everything is working properly. Faith in the airlines binds you to what you desire to do, reach your destination. The Pathfinder Resiliency Tool provides a unified-focused resiliency by helping you identify the direction you want to go (see figure 2). Ultimately, your meaning in life mediates the feeling state that you desire.

Efficacy of Meaning

The search for meaning is what drives us, but the efficacy of meaning is important in understanding its relationship to resiliency.[12] Efficacy of meaning is not just something significant to you, such as a feeling state, but it effectively results in a unified-focused, resilient, greater goal as well.

I love to run. I've been a runner all my life, but I can't make a living out of it. Same with coffee. I love to drink good coffee, but making a living as a barista won't put my five kids through college. These aspects of meaningfulness are helpful to my conditions-based resiliency, in that running (a values-based routine) keeps me healthy and drinking coffee in the morning makes me happy and lively. They are supportive values-based routines that are meaningful and notable. However, they are not efficacious enough as my primary purpose-role that forwards my life to the ultimate goal I'm trying to reach.

Efficacy is an important concept in regard to meaning and resiliency. It's when we deepen, develop, and diversify our meaning(s) in life to such an extent that if we experience a tragic

---

[12] Roy F. Baumeister, *Meanings of Life* (New York, NY: Guilford Press, 1991), 41.

loss, we can pivot to something else that is available for us to be or do. Resilient conditions make meanings that are efficacious.

Everything Is Meaningless

The Resiliency Unlimited paradox is this: we need meaning in life like we need oxygen, but everything is meaningless. In light of eternity, everything is meaningless. This is what Solomon says: "Meaningless. Meaningless. Everything is meaningless" (Ecclesiastes 1:1–2). Saying this is not being fatalistic. No one can predict the future and tell you the world is going to be just fine after you die. If history is a predictor of trends, we should be cautiously pessimistic.

This does not stop us from searching for positive meaning. We cannot deny this urge. We automatically desire within ourselves an ideal future self and an ideal life for our children. But at the end of the day, all the faith in external structures, people, and ourselves are not going to be good enough. It is faith in the living God that will never fail us and will welcome us into eternity.

My experience in the military has taught me that meaninglessness manifests when people experience serious threats or losses about that which is significant, the ultimate that we desire. Untold numbers of people become suicidal. I have seen this on too many occasions in my Army career, from the highest-ranking officers to the lowest enlisted soldiers. If one's identity is *only* drawn from what one does, the significance of certain relationships, or values-based routines, one can move into catastrophic meaning loss. If you put all your faith in a human institution and it systemically fails you, anxiety and depression is sure to emerge. That's why Solomon says, "It's all meaningless." You can't take it with you, but you can enjoy it for what it is.

Regardless, keep standing in your faith and spiritual identity no matter what.

Our hearts won't stop searching for meaning, but St. Augustine said it best: "Our heart is restless until it finds it's rest in Thee, O God." *The Heidelberg Catechism* teaches us through its question and answer pedagogy. "Question: What is your only comfort in life and death? Answer: That I am not my own, but belong with body and soul, and both in life and in death, to my faithful Savior, Jesus Christ."[13] To be as resilient as possible, our identity must be found in the voice of God, who speaks to our soul.

---

[13] Allen O. Miller and M. Eugene Osterhaven, trans., *The 400ʰ Anniversary Edition of the Heidelberg Catechism*, (Cleveland, OH: United Church Press, 1962), 9.

5

The Five IDEAS that Impact Your Life Without Your Permission

There is a famous children's book by the title, "Alexander and the Terrible, Horrible, No Good, Very Bad Day." Sometimes, we do have such a day or even a season of life. No one can stop the effects of these five: injustice, death, evil, absurdity, and suffering (IDEAS). We are all going to feel the impact of meaning loss from them, even if the core of our PSI is found in our relationship with God. When my wife and I got word she had cancer, I wasn't feeling cheerful. I was still anxious and sad, until we had a plan. When Christ was suffering death on the cross, he said, "Why have you forsaken me?" I believe he meant that in the core of his humanity, but he had hope.

Your faith identity in God is what ultimately provides the best source to remain hopeful. Having said this, no one volunteers for these IDEAS, but we all experience them without our permission. I'm not talking about heroes acting out of altruistic duty and incurring suffering. These are ideas that change, disrupt, and transition us. These IDEAS come to us from both natural disasters and man-made mistakes. When these IDEAS arrive in our life in clustered conditions, like in the book of Job, it may cause us to question our deepest-held convictions.

This is why I have created Resilience Unlimited, to help you find your best path on your worst day! What are you going to do when it happens? How are you going to react? How can you get ahead of the worst-case scenario? Most importantly, what do you need to believe that can withstand inevitable tragedy?

> Notice the spiritual compass in the bottom right-hand corner. It is through the use of your spiritual intelligence and a deepened, developed, and diversified PRT Meaning Map that will help you always find your best path. These resources provide robust pathways so that you can be as resilient as possible.

Figure 7

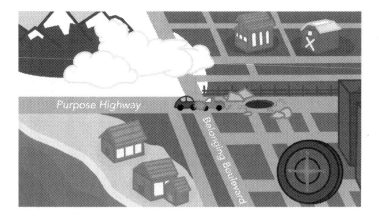

Injustice. No one wants to be violated. No one wants to be involuntarily subjected to criticism based on race, color, gender, or creed. Everyone experiences injustice—everyone. Just read the book of Psalms. They are written for us. Although we are all created equal in the eyes of God, human beings around the world oppress one another. It's not just an American problem. If you keep abreast of world history, you will find that injustice goes back to the beginning. Ought civilization improve and progress? I definitely think so. Tell that to the forces on both sides of the current war in Europe.

Death. There is no escape. Sometimes it's predictable. Other times it's not. Especially when it happens unpredictably, it's the most difficult to handle. When death occurs around us, our life changes. Boundaries are dissolved. We are thrust into a new meaning zone. A gap emerges. It becomes transition time without a visible end. All the grief emotions either show up or are being blocked out in an unhealthy way.

Evil. We are living in unprecedented times of evil in the United States. There's no room to think we can live in a Pollyanna world. A brief reflection on recent public maladies confronts us with the phrase *Evil is crouching at our door.* We can act like a sheepdog; it doesn't stop wolves from being wolves.

Absurdity. I define this for the pathfinder as the unwelcomed, unexpected halting or breakdown of human or mechanistic systems. This is Murphy's Law. Anything that can break down will break down. It happens when we are moving toward our goal. It's disruptive and very frustrating.

Suffering. All of us are going to suffer in life. It doesn't matter how rich we are. Money can't buy our way out of pain. We can't eat, drink, sleep, drug, or completely work out the pain with exercise. Pain and suffering come with our neurological package. Whether it's physical or mental suffering, both show up in the same part of the brain where pain is located.

As you scan the above IDEAS, you will notice that all of them are akin to physical threats. I'm calling them external negative factors (ENFs). There is a physicality component about them. Later, the psychological will be addressed. The ENFs are object forms or categories of distress. It is important to note for later how these ENFs will be addressed under the meaning marker spiritual intelligence.

Why are these IDEAS important to itemize for the Pathfinder Resiliency Tool? They can prevent us from reaching our goals. They can hamper our ability to be resilient. Thus, itemizing them will help you find your best path on your worst day. There is a neurological component that is important to understand in all this.

6

The Neuroscience of a
Unified-Focused Resiliency

Our brains need a unifying framework for managing life conditions (purpose, belonging, values-based routines, and spiritual intelligence) toward the desired ideal future self. When you and I move with respect to achieving goals in an unhindered manner, we experience positive emotions through the dopaminergic system. Dopamine is a neurochemical that promotes reward. If you are achieving your goals, you feel better. If you are prevented from doing this, you feel worse. This is oversimplifying it, but at an elementary level, this is how we operate.

Entropy is disordered events that prevent someone from reaching their goals. To put it clearly, it's essentially a breakdown of what is desired. This is the IDEAS at work. It stops us from experiencing dopamine. The physical entropy of the IDEAS leads to a psychological entropy.

See figure 7. Life feels good when you have a plan for a great day at work, until you have a car accident while driving there, or your computer no longer works, or you crack your phone and it becomes dysfunctional.

Issues like this are inevitable. It sends us into what Stanford University neuroscientist Dr. Andrew Huberman calls "a dopamine trough." We then feel anxious and depressed. Stress hormones are released because we can't get to our goals. However, we experience a dopamine wave when we are finding our best path, reaching our goals. Huberman emphasizes that we are regularly cycling through waves and troughs.[14]

The Resiliency Unlimited definition of *resiliency* is finding your best path. Neuroscience has important educational implications to the point of resiliency. Knowing you are going to experience waves and troughs in dopamine, you can be strategic by intra-coordinating the Seven Meaning-Making Markers. You can strategize a unified-focused resiliency. It brings the important markers and goals into focus. This is something you will do in Part II, when you write this on your PRT Meaning Map.

This might seem complex on the surface since there are many uncontrollable variables at play. There is an old saying: "If you shoot for the moon and miss, at least you hit the stars." We have already established that we are goal (*telos*) oriented. We are always running ahead. Harnessing your attention to focus on the most valuable, in the ultimate sense, is important as you ponder preventive resiliency.

Know the Pattern to Always Find Your Best Path

So when entropy occurs, what can you do to find your best path as soon as possible? Know the pattern. The entropy event becomes a meaning gap (figure 5) that sends you into a dopamine trough. The dopamine trough, through the meaning gap, can send you into a negative self-identity narrative. Clusters of the IDEAS can send you into catastrophic meaning loss. Recognizing this now can help you find your best path on your worst day.

---

[14] Dr. Andrew Huberman, "Leveraging Dopamine to Overcome Procrastination and Optimize Effort," in *The Huberman Podcast*, podcast, March 27, 2023.

This is psycho-spiritual, preventive, educational resiliency. It's ready-resilience.

A biblical example is the story of Elijah. He must have been on a spiritual high after he called down fire from heaven. After that, he then slaughtered the 450 priests of Baal at the Kishon Brook—dopamine wave. Then his life was gravely threatened by Jezebel, and he fled for his survival—dopamine trough. He told God, "It is enough now; O Lord, take away my life, for I am no better than my fathers" (1 Kings 19:4). This was a suicidal ideation, a request to die. He told God that he was all alone. However, through the voice of God, he received spiritual perspective. He understood that his conditions were not as bad. God told him that, indeed, he was not alone. There were others with him. His positive self-identity returned with this new understanding.

Here's the point: we read the story as an outsider and see the big picture. God was taking care of him all along. You are going to face gaps and troughs. You will have scripts of NSI like Christ on the cross. But this is the message for you: God has not left you alone.

The Resilience Unlimited—Pathfinder Resiliency Tool distinction in resiliency is that you leverage your spiritual intelligence, your true identity. For many in our growing culture, this is an untapped resource. It is with your values and virtues that you bring to bear spiritual solutions against entropy. Spiritual intelligence frames the way you collectively maneuver the resources in your conditions (see figure 2) and find your best path. This is the answer to meaninglessness and character fragility. Developing this is akin to wisdom.

7

The Pathfinder Resiliency Tool Is Your Warrior Code

I n all contexts and segments of society, whether good or bad, children, young men, and women are socialized with a narrative of values and virtues. It's impossible not to have some kind of moral, ethical, narrative structure to help us make sense of the world by what is right and wrong. The Pathfinder Resiliency Tool serves as mediator to aid in clarifying the narrative that defines your life. Have you morally and ethically arrived in life? I will think not. Should you be willing to change? Do you have a growth mindset? We can all improve and grow in care, love, mind, spirit, respect, and protection of what is the good, true, and beautiful.

There is a special culture in the American military defined by its own values. Some of it is explicitly formatted in military doctrine, and other concepts are carried around in tattoos. Today, statistics show that fewer military families are encouraging their children to serve the country in uniform. The recruiting challenge is the worst since the Vietnam era. There's a sense of meaningless that pervades America, and it's lined with character fragility.

During the years of the global war on terror, there were several sources of inspiration capturing what was going on in the culture. The authors brought out what was present and needed during that era. The idea of a warrior code can reinvigorate resiliency health where character fragility is present. Steven Pressfield, a distinguished writer and military author, opines on the topic of the *warrior ethos*.

> The Warrior Ethos is taught. On the football field in Topeka, in the mountains of the Hindu Kush, on the lion-infested plains of Kenya and Tanzania. Courage is modeled for the youth by fathers and older brothers, by mentors and elders. It is inculcated, in almost all cultures, by a regimen of training and discipline. This discipline frequently culminates in an ordeal of initiation. The Spartan youth receives his shield, the paratrooper is awarded his wings, the Afghan boy is handed his AK-47.[15]

In the book *Faith of the American Soldier*, Stephen Mansfield also provides analysis and testimony of what it means to live out a warrior code.

> The warrior code takes a soldier and makes him a knight. It connects the natural life of a fighter to a supernatural understanding of the warrior calling. His duties are transformed into holy sacrifices; his sense of self is reformed into an image of the servant in pursuit of valor. He becomes part of a fellowship, a noble tradition

---

[15] Steven Pressfield, *The Warrior Ethos* (New York, NY: Black Irish Press, 2011), 14–15.

that flows through him and carries him beyond
the mediocre and the vain.[16]

The challenge of our culture today is that we are missing these above essential elements; we are weaker as a society. Dr. Harold Koenig, psychiatrist at Duke University and a leading expert in evidenced-based spirituality and military spiritual readiness, has raised awareness on the effects of meaninglessness and character fragility on our American fighting forces. In *Spiritual Readiness: Essentials for Military Leaders and Chaplains*, Koenig et al. write:

> What is missing here is a full understanding of the spiritual significance and importance of what members of our militaries are risking their lives for. How many Sailors, Marines, Coasties, Soldiers, and Aviators fight to defend the greater good against forces that would overcome it and destroy justice? Such purpose enables the warrior to fight with their spirit. Might the lack of such a powerful spiritual motivation be responsible for the growing mental, social, behavioral, and even physical problems that are now epidemic among members of the U.S. Armed Forces (and to some degree among members of the armed forces of their allies)? Might the absence of such spiritual purpose affect the desire to fight, the deep and sustained will necessary to overcome sometimes daunting obstacles in dangerous and often life-threating situations?[17]

---

[16] Stephen Mansfield, *The Faith of the American Soldier* (Lake Mary, FL: Charisma House, 2005), 116.

[17] Harold G. Koenig, MD; Lindsay B. Carey, PhD; and Faten Al Zaben, MD, *Spiritual Readiness: Essentials for Military Leaders and Chaplains* (Las Vegas, NV: 2022), 5.

Whether you are military or a civilian, the Pathfinder Resiliency Tool provides an opportunity for you to more clearly define the narrative in which you believe and live. Everyone is in a spiritual war. I assert that the PRT can be a mediator of a warrior code for a culture that is both fragile and meaningless. The PRT redefines your future story. It can deepen your spiritual connection to give you greater conviction. Our world needs people of conviction and character. How might you capture new meanings and essence of life that can motivate and fuel you to live for the sake of others, to selflessly serve, and to help improve the world we live?

PART II

Practical Application of
Pathfinder Resiliency
Tool Meaning Map

I

Purpose: Developing Your Target

W hen I train using the curriculum Resilience Unlimited—Pathfinder Resiliency Tool in person, I start with the three pillars of meaning (see figure 3): purpose, belonging, and values-based routines. This seems to be the best place to start.

Simon Sinek has a convincing argument with thirteen million views at TEDxPugetSound. "Start with why. How great leaders inspire action."[18] Your why drives you into purpose.

There is an important existential question that has been asked in different ways. "Whoever has a why to live for can bear almost any how." When I provided this quote to soldiers, it immediately resonates with them. They are looking for their why. Almost all of them have no idea that it's attributed to the nineteenth-century German philosopher Friedrich Nietzsche.

The aphorism stands as self-evident. There is evidenced-based research that says having a sense of purpose leads to

---

[18] Simon Sinek, "Start with Why—How Great Leaders Inspire Action," YouTube video, 2009, https://www.youtube.com/watch?v=u4ZoJKF VuA&t=11s. Simon Sinek is internationally known as an advisor in leadership and business.

longevity in life.[19] We naturally search for this. Purpose is a part of meaning. It answers the why question. Evidenced-based reviews about purpose say that it is essential for well-being and provides resistance to anxiety and depression.

Having studied much of the literature by psychologists on purpose, I want to provide a definition that is relevant to Resilience Unlimited. Purpose is a personal vision of one's life whereby tasks and responsibilities are moving oneself toward a projected end state. Elements of care, commitment, and risk make it meaningful. Personal awareness of purpose in life brings a sense of satisfaction. Purpose moves toward a vision. When purpose incorporates the good of the world, it's wired with more intrinsic value. It's not just *your* purpose but also for some greater good.

Soldiers given the task and purpose of regularly picking up trash, a "police call," generally becomes a nonstarter. Yes, it makes the world beautiful when it's cleaner. However, the menial and mundane nature of regularly doing it seems to diminish care and commitment, and it's missing the zest of risk. To strive after purpose that is just out of your comfort range makes it feel more meaningful.

To develop your target of purpose, I have laid out three different exercises. First, I recommend taking an Enneagram assessment. (You can review the 9-Type Personality Indicator on the Trekk Unlimited website, www.trekkunlimited.com.) On your PRT Meaning Map, this is located under your Profile

---

[19] Dr. Robert Butler, "Huge Study Confirms Purpose and Meaning Add Years to Your Life," https://www.bluezones.com/2019/05/news-huge-study-confirms-purpose-and-meaning-add-years-to-life/.

Range. Second, take the Discover Your Core Purpose exercise. Third, develop a personal Purpose Statement.

What About the Enneagram?

Personality theory is a cottage industry. Resilience Unlimited is not joining it. However, having professionally studied, taken, and provided personality assessments, from the 567-question Minnesota Multiphasic Personality Inventory (MMPI) to Mark Gungor's Flag Page, I believe people want to understand themselves. It's helpful.

To quote a tweet by Dr. Adam Grant, business psychology professor at the University of Pennsylvania, on March 5, 2023, "Personality types are a myth. Each trait exists on a continuum shaped like a bell curve." This is a necessary caveat to introduce the Enneagram. If you decide to engage the Enneagram, notice that your personality is flexible on the continuum. This means it may not feel hard and fast. You can be a little of this and a little of that. These are some important generalizations that provide keen insights. I am not about to preach the Enneagram gospel. It's a recommendation.

Briefly, there are three things I want to tell you about this initial step. First, it is highly affirmed by a well-respected evangelical pastor and theologian, Dr. James Emery White of Mecklenburg Community Church in Charlotte, North Carolina. He provides solid historical evidence that the assessment originates from the Syrian Christian monk named Evagrius Ponticus. Dr. White summarizes its unmistakable ancient Christian origins and early use.[20] He also provided a well-grounded podcast on

[20] Dr. James Emery White, "What to Make of the Enneagram," https://www.crosswalk.com/blogs/dr-james-emery-white/what-to-make-of-the-enneagram.html. Dr. James Emery White is the former President of Gordon-Conwell Theological Seminary.

the subject and a sermon series called "Finding Your Way to You: The Bible, the Enneagram and Self-Understanding." These are trustworthy resources to learn about its background.

Second, what is the intent of taking the Enneagram? It will help you discover your core desires and fears—in other words, your core values and what you avoid. In understanding your purpose in life, you want to sense what you are gravitating toward. You also want to be cognizant of what you naturally avoid doing. When you think about the idea that you are already a pathfinder, always running ahead, you want to assist yourself in the direction that feels most organic to you. You want to discover your why.

Third, I don't have another recommendation of personality assessments for the Pathfinder Resiliency Tool. However, you may find an exception as it helps you develop your own purpose in life. As you understand Resilience Unlimited—Pathfinder Resiliency Tool and learn about your Enneagram type, you will find that it is a very fitting personality assessment. There is a plethora of information on the Enneagram. You can spend a lot of time on it. You don't need to become an expert. The intent is to get to know yourself in understanding your core desires and core fears.

Complete step 1 of your Pathfinder Resiliency Tool Meaning Map by assessing yourself at www.trekkunlimited. com, or there are many different versions on the internet, which some have a cost. There are books that provide a version as well. I'm not recommending any in particular. Write the results on your PRT Meaning Map. By the way, I am an Enneagram 7, the Enthusiast, with my Core Desire being passion and my Core Fear is being confined.

PRT Core Purpose Exercise

Understand your PRT core purpose (figure 8). This is a much simpler process. This graph looks like the many *ikigai* exercises that are all over the internet. *Ikigai* is the Japanese word for "purpose."

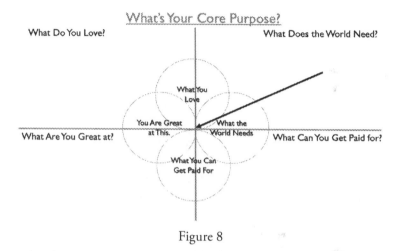

What's Your Core Purpose?

Figure 8

Take your information from the Enneagram and begin to assimilate it into this process as background situational awareness. Answer the questions in this quad chart. Write as many answers as you can in each one. Then circle the number one in each quad that you feel most emphatic. You gravitate toward these. After that, put them all together in one sentence: For example, "My core purpose is to train people around the world who want to become resilient." Write your core purpose on your PRT Meaning Map.

I want to share with you a frequently asked question that I get about the Pathfinder Resiliency Tool. "Can my core purpose [or other parts of the PRT Meaning Map] be aspirational?" The answer is yes! Think of care, commitment, and risk. What are you caring about? What are you willing to commit to? Do you need to muster up the courage to take a calculated risk for it? Since we are always running ahead, in navigational language, you are plotting a point from your PRT Meaning Map to your horizon of hope. This is how you deepen, develop, and diversify yourself. One further caveat: I recognize some people do not have current conditions that allow there to be financial gains ("What can I get paid for?"), like a stay-at home-mother. Even so, what other kinds of capital can be gained besides money? Think of future capital, social capital, or creative capital of other means.

The PRT Purpose-in-Life Statement

Here's a quick review of the PRT definition of *purpose*: Purpose is a personal vision of one's life whereby tasks and responsibilities are moving oneself toward a projected end state. An element of risk makes it meaningful. Personal awareness of purpose in life brings a sense of satisfaction. Purpose moves toward a vision. When purpose incorporates the good of the world, it's wired with more intrinsic value. It's not just *your* purpose but also for some greater good.

With this in mind and to build on the first two parts of Purpose-in-Life, answer these questions by filling in the blank. Write this on your PRT Meaning Map.

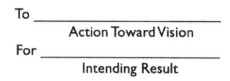

To _____
Action Toward Vision

For _____
Intending Result

Figure 9

Here's my purpose-in-life statement as an example: "To train people to be more resilient, adventure in life, and care for my family." You will notice that it says *to* and *for*. *To* is the action. And *for* is the intended result. This is what gets me out of bed in the morning. This is what excites me. I want to help people find their best path in life.

You can write this in different ways; however, you want to say it in a way that is easy to remember. What motivates you? Your purpose-in-life statement is something that speaks to you when you pull out your PRT Meaning Map. You can possibly feel an eternal *yes*.

Anxiety About Your Target

If you ever pointed something to shoot at a target, the initial experience can feel tense. You are developing your target in your first purpose statement. Relax. If it doesn't completely fit, you can restate it again, and again. Plus, your life is always in draft. Who you are today and what you desire to become will contextually change over time. This is why the PRT is a tool for life. It can grow with you because you are moving into your future. Entropy happens, but we are always running ahead. The PRT Meaning Map is a mediator for personal growth.

2

Belonging: Setting Your Circles of Trust

C ommonly attributed as an African proverb is this quote: "If you want to go fast in life, go alone. If you want to go far in life, go with a friend." This was the principle that helped me have a rewarding long day running (double-crossing) the Grand Canyon R3. I was successful because I didn't go alone. Without my two runner friends, I would be physically and psychologically less secure attempting this act of personal endurance. What area in your personal journey in life do you need or desire others to be a pathfinder with you?

Belonging starts with a *longing* to *be* with others. Belonging occurs when others return this longing back to you. From cradle to grave, we need attachment, connection, and belonging to others. Currently, what is being reported and experienced today is that young people have never been lonelier.[21] The Gallup organization reported in January of 2023 that there is a silent global pandemic of loneliness. The US Surgeon General has written extensively on this.[22]

---

[21] Nana Baah, "Young People Are Lonelier than Ever," *Vice*, April 22, 2022.
[22] Vivek H. Murthy, Together, the Healing Power of Connection in a Sometimes Lonely World, (New York, NY: Harper Collins, 2020)

Over three hundred million people globally don't have a single friend and 20 percent of adults don't have a friend to count on in a time of need. Isolation and loneliness bring with it risk of serious health factors.[23] Nearly one in five American men report they do not have a single friend.[24]

In my experience as an Army Chaplain, the number one reason why soldiers attempt or commit suicide is the loss of a relationship. This isn't a US Army problem. This is a Western world problem as we know it. It all revolves around meaning. Resiliency is finding your best path to deepen, develop, and diversify the meaning of your relationships.

To use the analogy of relationships as a healthy human cell, it should be semipermeable. Good things can flow in and bad things can't, to put it simply. A healthy cell regulates what flows in and out. An impermeable cell will dry up and die. Human beings need healthy semipermeable relationships in order to be resilient.

I want to introduce you to the Dunbar Circle. Dr. Robin Dunbar of Oxford University proposes the science behind optimal relationships in his book *How Many Friends Does One Person Need?*[25] It doesn't matter if you have a million Instagram or TikTok followers; you can only truly know about 150 people. We can only handle so many real personal relationships. There are only so many hours in a day. Significant belonging-in-life relationships take time and effort.

---

[23] https://www.cdc.gov/aging/publications/features/lonely-older-adults.html.

[24] https://nypost.com/2021/07/07/friendship-recession-15-of-men-are-without-a-close-pal/.

[25] Robin Dunbar, *How Many Friends Does One Person Need, Dunbar's Number and Other Evolutionary Quirks*, (Cambridge: MA, Harvard University Press, 2010).

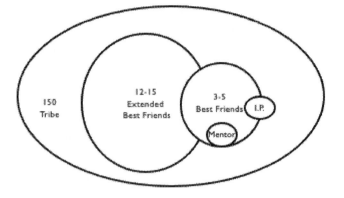

Figure 10

Now look at your PRT Meaning Map (figure 6) on the right-hand side, where the belonging pillar is located. You will begin to identity who your potential tribe can be, extended best friends, your three to five best friends, a possible mentor, and your intimate partner—if you have a spouse, boyfriend, or girlfriend.

Frequently asked question: "What if I don't have three to five best friends?" You might not. It seems rare today, but those who do are more resilient in life. As has been said before, your life is in draft, and so is your PRT Meaning Map. Don't sweat the start. Just begin. You will have a lifetime of opportunity to make this condition of resiliency stronger.

Tribe (150 people): Believe it or not, your tribe has a potentially greater protective factor for your well-being than an intimate partner.[26] Think about it. When you have one egg in one basket and that egg shatters, what do you have? When you have a tribe available when your most significant egg shatters, you can be resilient by finding your best path forward again. What tribe(s) do you already belong to? Do you belong to a religious organization, nonprofit, civic organization, team, affinity club, gym membership, or internet group? You might have overlapping tribes of relationships.

This is what's important about choosing or identifying with a particular tribe: they should share the same unified-focused resiliency values as you (see figure 2). Are they going to help you get where you want to go? Do they hold similar beliefs as you? Are you going to help them as well? If you experience one of the IDEAS, can someone from your tribe be there for you? Write in what tribes you belong to on your PRT Meaning Map.

What's the definition of a friend? I want to propose two answers to you that come from my military experience and my marriage therapy background. First is the statement "I've got your back." This is what it means to have a friend or a best friend. You know that he or she will have your back. They will stand up for you. They will stand by you. They will tell you the honest truth in love. They will tell you if you are right. They will tell you if you are wrong. They will fight alongside you. Second, they will support you on your worst day or worst night. They will say, "I will be there for you." And they do it. This is true belonging.

Extended Best Friends (12–15 people): These are not

---

[26] Olga Stavrova and Maike Luhmann, "Social Connectedness as a Source and Consequence of Meaning in Life," *Journal of Positive Psychology* 11, no. 5 (September 2016): 477.

your besties, but they are in a social category where they share their lives with you and yours with them, just not in the most vulnerable ways. I call this group extended best friends because your life is always in draft. When my family and I would move around the country every couple of years, we would get close with people for a time and have to move over one thousand miles away. Sometimes relationships have a way of cycling back again, and you pick up where you have left off.

Someone in your extended best friend (EBF) group could move to become part of your three to five best friends. I know some best friend relationships can be sacred. But keep in mind that we live in a fluid culture where people come and go. Someone can move into your EBF group and move out. This is the point: cultivate relationships. Resiliency is dependent on the present conditions of relationships. Have you ever been left in a lurch? To find your best path on your worst day, experiencing the IDEAS, you need close friends in your life.

Three to Five Best Friends: When I talk about the three to five best friends in training, it feels very intimidating to many people. Our world is struggling. Hallmarks of best friendships reveal vulnerability to each other, accountability, validation, and support. That is why I developed the very wooden-like Best Friend Pledge so that you can have a handle on how to develop this.

Best Friend Pledge

1. I invite you to be one of my top five friends so we can create a strong relationship and mutually support each other's success.
2. We will talk regularly during the month.
3. We will be vulnerable to each other in a time of need.
4. I will have your back, and you will have mine. We will be *there* for each other when it really matters.

5. If we know that the other is in need, we will frequently call or visit.
6. If I cannot keep this pledge, I will provide courtesy and inform the other.

Who can be your three to five best friends? Write this on your PRT Meaning Map.

Mentor: I have a mentor. Throughout my life, I've been blessed to have several at different times and locations. It makes a big difference, especially when it comes to resiliency. When I found out my wife was diagnosed with cancer, the first people I shared it with were my best friends and my mentor. They all prayed for me. It was my mentor who said some unforgettable, wise words that were exactly what I needed to hear.

There are different kinds of mentors whom you might list for yourself: a pastor, a therapist, a chaplain, an advanced leader, a financial adviser, or a wiser person who has some age and distance from you. Your mentor won't be a best friend. This is a person who can give you sage advice that you can't get from a best friend. If you don't have one already, who can be your mentor? Write this on your PRT Meaning Map.

Intimate Partner: Your intimate partner is the person with whom you are likely to experience the highest level of vulnerability. This is the person you let in your life to be your biggest fan but also has the greatest potential to hurt you. This relationship has the most significance in relation to the condition of your resiliency. If you have a spouse, boyfriend, or girlfriend, write it on your PRT Meaning Map.

3

Values-Driven Routines:
Fueling the Machine

L ast time I checked Amazon, it revealed over fifty thousand books about habits. This is not going to be one more. However, as a meaning-making marker, your habits are *very* significant. Therefore, it needs to be properly addressed.

James Clear, the author of *Atomic Habits*, said it best when he was on *The Carey Nieuwhof Leadership Podcast*: "The big picture is that I think your habits matter, not just because of the results that they get you, but because of the identity that they reinforce. So your habits are how you embody a particular identity."[27] His statement can be summarized more succinctly by saying it this way: values-driven habits reinforce the identity one desires.

In Resilience Unlimited—Pathfinder Resiliency Tool, values-based routines are those informed and guided by one's spiritual intelligence (ethics, morals, and spiritual beliefs). Values-based

---

[27] James Clear, "James Clear on the Backstory behind *Atomic Habits*, His Top Tips on Habit Formation, Values, Identity, and His Theory on Selling More than Ten Million Copies of *Atomic Habits*," in *The Carey Nieuwhof Leadership Podcast*, podcast, January 2, 2023.

routines fuel one's purpose and belonging. Values-based routines show up as habits, disciplines, rituals, and traditions that motivate and fuel you to reach your ideal future self.

Indeed, the Christian identity is the one first received; however, it is not the only identity we carry inside us or display. We have career identities and social identities. I can't be a chaplain without an army, a husband without my wife, a father without my children, a runner unless I run. To keep relationships strong and resilient to others and myself, there must be maintenance to it. I need to clarify my boundaries. Values-based routines are concerned with the location of boundaries and what is included, excluded, or neglected. Values-based routines set the boundaries to our desired identity.

Dr. John Gottman, one of the most renowned marriage therapists and a practicing Jew, has much import here. His evidenced-based therapy system has influenced the development of the Resilient Unlimited model. He suggests to "Create Shared Meaning" through habits, disciplines, rituals, and traditions. He advocates "spiritual dimensions that have to do with creating an inner life together—a culture rich with symbols and rituals, and appreciation for your roles and goals that link you, that lead you to understand what it means to be a part of the family you have become."[28]

On my deployment to Kosovo in 2014, I was invited to a Christmas Eve celebration with the Polish Battalion. I unsuspectingly walked into a building that looked like a dingy warehouse on the outside, but on the inside, it was transformed into a glorious atmosphere of decorations, rich in symbols, delicious holiday food, incredible music, costumes, and a traditional re-telling of the birth of Christ. It was all in polish. I was the only

[28] John M. Gottman, PhD, and Nan Silver, *The Seven Principles for Making Marriage Work: A Practical Guide from the Country's Foremost Relationship Expert* (New York, NY: Three Rivers Press, 1999), 243–44.

American there. In a country far from home, I was blown away by the significance of all of this joyful meaning harnessed together in one place. I learned that it is the intentional regular doing of significant things together with rituals and symbols that make meaning happen. Overall, it's our values-based routines that establishes boundaries to give us confidence and hope as it fuels purpose and belonging.

What it Takes to Find Your Best Path

When you think about what your ideal future self looks like, what will it take you to get there? What do you need to do in regard to values-based routines? To return to what James K. A. Smith said, "[W]hat makes us who we are, the kind of people we are—is what we love." What we care about shapes our future. Our routines must be connected to our values, and our values must be connected to our routines.

When you look at figure 2, the quality of your personal and family health in the conditions is dependent on values-based routines. These conditions are your relationships, career development and progression, self-care (sleep, exercise, sacred rest, nutrition, and finances), and recreation.

Saying you want to be physically fit is different than doing it. If you don't make the changes by aligning the stated value, actual routines to the time-driven-demarcating boundaries, then you are probably just deceiving yourself. Something else is actually more important. I'm not talking about perfection. This is Resilience Unlimited—How to Always Find Your Best Path. If you don't make a commitment to it, it's likely not going to start all by itself. The Pathfinder Resiliency Tool is the mechanism to keep yourself accountable to your ideal future self.

I like the Latin term that St. Augustine is known to have used, *ordo amoris* (order your loves). This phrase reminds me of a time I was interviewing a couple, and I was told that the husband liked to play three hours of video games after work every night. He would play more, but his wife protested. If you want a working relationship or a growing career, you need to order priorities.

To be proficient in your career or relationships it takes values-based routines. When I was deployed to Kosovo our unit conducted peacetime airborne operations, parachuting out of Black Hawk helicopters. One day I walked into a NATO ally office, who were watching videos of this. Soldiers from that country were remarking very loudly to themselves about the proficiency of the paratroopers and the Black Hawks. They loved watching this. It takes highly trained, disciplined, and physically fit paratroopers and pilots to execute these maneuvers. Everything is carefully choreographed. It looks awesome, but there is so much invisible work that goes on behind the scenes to get there.

As a Brigade Chaplain for the Fourth Infantry Division, I remember the Sustainment Brigade Commander drilling into us how important it was to do things routinely. "It's like mowing the lawn," he would say. "You can't let it go. It will get out of control." You need to keep up with maintenance and fuel the machines. World wars are won through the maintenance of its war machines and logistical operations. I regularly stood in briefings about the supply chain for Black Hawk helicopters and M1 Abrams tanks. National security depends on an imperceptible system to sustain them. What you desire in your ideal future self is hidden in a productive struggle that no one sees. Your hidden values-based routines have big payoffs in the public. You will reach your ideal future self only if you prioritize values-driven routines. They fuel your purpose and belonging to build conditions-based resiliency.

Look at your PRT Meaning Map. In the center, you can see an area that provides a list of your top seven values-based routines. Remember: your life is always in draft. What might you need to prioritize? At this juncture, I want you to refrain from fully completing this section. It is after the next meaning-making marker, Positive Self-Identity (PSI), that I want you to fill it in. In your PSI, you are going to specifically write out the vision for yourself. After that, write out your values-based routines to help you reach your ideal future self and avoid your worst future self. You will also notice boxes with indicating letters: *D, W, M,* and *S.* This means routines done daily, weekly, monthly, or seasonally. Check the box that will keep yourself aligned with your ideal future self and horizon of hope.

4

Spiritual Intelligence:
One Compass to Rule Them All

In *Crime and Punishment*, Fyodor Dostoyevsky wrote, "It takes something more than intelligence to act intelligently." Spirituality is the fundamental feature of this resiliency training. In our Western traditional presuppositions, spirituality has been greatly marginalized. Many want to keep it there. Logically, when comprehensive resiliency is studied among all the other domains such as physical, mental, social, financial, and spiritual, one will think that they all can be integrated together. This is not the case.

Can you integrate mental and physical? Yes. Social and financial? Yes. What about physical or other domains into spiritual? These domains of resiliency can influence the spiritual, but do not truly integrate with it. However, one can take a spiritual worldview and integrate it into all those other domains: how to be physically fit, socially relevant, mentally stable, and financially solvent. This is why understanding spiritual resiliency is the most important!

To be maximally resilient in all the domains, it takes spiritual intelligence. Spiritual intelligence as a particular field of study is a growing concept. Perhaps Resilience Unlimited can contribute some to this. A working definition of *spiritual intelligence* that is helpful to start with is from Harris Wiseman and Fraser Watts. It's defined as "an adaptive intelligence which enables people to develop their values, vision, and capacity for meaning."[29]

The spiritual intelligence you have is from values you hold and the virtues you live and practice. Values are what you believe. Virtues are the good attitudes and behaviors you exhibit. Everyone has beliefs. All practice faith, as already explained when examining meaning. Your primary meaning is your religion.

When it comes to spiritual intelligence, there are generally only two modes of relating to spirituality. Either you relate to a transcendent higher power, God, or you engage in transcendental practices to cope with life. Some have a combination of both. Whether you are a Christian, Muslim, Jew, Hindu, or other and have a theistic understanding of God or an atheist or agnostic who practices meditation, yoga, and so forth, you are engaging in spiritual practices that become indicated in cortical thickness of the brain. MRI brain scans have proved this. This cortical thickness is a biological buffer to anxiety and depression.

The Data is Undeniable

The science of spirituality is an incontrovertibly growing field of evidenced-based research. Some on the leading edge are duly noted here. Lisa Miller, PhD, psychologist and professor at Columbia University and author of *The Awakened Brain* (2021) and *The Spiritual Child* (2016), has been showcased around the world and trained the US Army. As cited earlier, a leading psychiatrist is Dr. Harold Koenig of Duke University. He has worked across all military branches. He's produced other volumes of evidenced-based research in this area. Two more of significance

---

[29] Harris Wiseman and Fraser Watts, "Spiritual Intelligence: Participating with Heart, Mind, and Body," Journal of Religion and Science, *Wiley Blackwell* (2022), https://doi.org/10.1111/zygo.12804.

to note are Tyler J. VanderWeele, PhD, and John R. Peteet, MD, of Harvard University, who have cowritten *Handbook of Religion and Health*, third edition (2021), with Dr. Koenig. Another leading psychiatrist is Dr. Andrew Newberg of Jefferson University Hospital in Philadelphia, who is also a professor at the University of Pennsylvania. He is the author of *Born to Believe* (2007) and *Won't Go Away* (2002). Psychologist David DeSteno, PhD, of Northeastern University in Boston recently released an important book, *How God Works: The Science behind the Benefits of Religion* (2021).

All the above scholars will argue or validate that we are wired for spirituality at birth. Dr. Lisa Miller delineates this pre-installed architecture of the brain as a spiritual docking station.[30] We neglect it to our detriment.

What does this all mean? I am not arguing that all religion is equal or the same. What I am saying is that there are tremendous benefits and protective factors related to resiliency via spirituality that have yet to fully reach the public square. Dr. Miller's research has penetrated some of the hallowed halls of our government and military. It is now widely reaching the marketplace.

In regard to resiliency, she articulates that a person who has a developed spiritual core, someone who is regularly practicing religion, is 80 percent less likely to become addicted, has a 70 percent protective factor against risk-taking, 60 percent less likely to be depressed, and 50 percent to over 80 percent less likely to commit suicide.[31] With an understanding of resiliency from statistics like this, it's time for a new health revolution by

---

[30] Lisa Miller, *The Awakened Brain: The New Science of Spirituality and Our Quest for an Inspired Life* (New York, NY: Random House, 2021), 8.

[31] Dr. Lisa Miller, "Core Science on Mental Health Prevention, H2F Spiritual Readiness Handbook," v. 6 (June 2022), in *The Spiritual Child: The New Science of Parenting for Health and Lifelong Thriving*, Lisa Miller (New York, NY: St. Martin's Press, 2016).

encouraging spiritual growth in clients and the public. Spiritual intelligence should lead the way.

Defining and regularly clarifying your spiritual intelligence in life provides focused direction of your purpose, belonging, and values-based routines so that you can get the most meaning and positive self-identity. When these conditions are present, it gives you a horizon of hope.

The Pathfinder Resiliency Tool Dialectic

Your life is a *dialectic*. This word is descriptive of conversations, standards, and opposites. We are always conversing with ourselves about the world we live in. There are standards within the world that we must measure up. There is the polarization of what we desire and what we eschew.

We need to plan, but our life is always in draft. We need to obey traffic laws, but we still speed a little. We can be weak and strong at the same time. We can be intellectually brilliant but still do dumb things. We can care too much about something, like drinking coffee, and disregard our conscience about overimbibing caffeine. We need meaning in life like we need oxygen, but everything is meaningless. We can exemplify both virtues and vices. We can know what is wrong and still do right and vice versa.

The Christian is both a saint and a sinner. The apostle Paul has written, "I want to do what is good, but I don't. I don't want to do what is wrong, but I do it anyway" (Romans 7:19). The paradox of God's presence is the accompanying feature of unflattering vulnerability. It's both shock and awe.

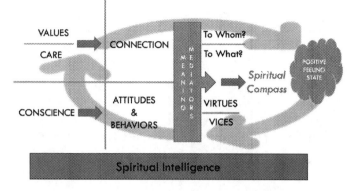

Figure 11

Don't let this model intimidate you. It is a dialectic that reflects not just parallel opposites but also a driving connection toward a *telos*, a meaning-end, which is the feeling state that we desire. Human beings are undeniably constructed to be emotional beings. We are always running ahead to the feeling state that we desire in the midst of a dialectical life.

Start with me in the top left-hand corner of the figure with *care*. All of us care about something and someone. It's impossible not to care at all. All of us care. It's fundamental to our humanity. What do you care about? Remember: what you care about shapes your future. What you care about is what you *value*. Care and value cause us to *connect* to something or someone. Having already discussed in the topic of meaning, those things/people are *mediators*. What do they mediate?

The mediators bind our lives to give us a *feeling state* we desire. This is our religion; the mediators that bind us to 'whom' and 'what'. Our worship comes from this part of us. In the purest sense, it is spiritual. It's what philosophers and theologians like Paul Tillich called "the Ultimate Concern," Karl Rhaner "the Absolute Mystery," and C. S. Lewis, "Longing for Joy."

In the New Testament, the apostle Paul writes, "For there is one God, and there is one mediator between God and men, the man Christ Jesus" (I Timothy 2:5). This is the Christian's ultimate compass, the Word incarnate. It's quite unlike Jack Sparrow's compass in *Pirates of the Caribbean*. His is a compass of his own desires. Sparrow's compass of desire is highly emblematic of our cultural moment. Carl Trueman's work *The Rise and Triumph of the Modern Self*[32] provides important historical sequencing for how we have arrived at our milieu where meaninglessness and fragility are at epidemic proportions.

Now on the bottom left-hand corner, we recognize that we all have a *conscience*, which dictates our *attitudes* and *behaviors*. The conscience engages with the mediators of the who and the what, and we mitigate our attitudes with *virtues* (goodness) or *vice* (badness). Whatever virtue or vice is expressed becomes the desired feeling state at the moment.

What I'm calling here the *spiritual compass* is the filtering mechanism through which we screen what we believe to be the moral, ethical, and spiritual. It is not just a compass, but this is where your warrior code is located. This is the narratives of beliefs that form your moral, ethical, spiritual, and religious content. Your spiritual compass and warrior code go together. What I'm describing here is the metaphysical. I'm just using metaphorical language to understand this phenomena.

The figure is unable to dimensionally express the complete dialectical (conversational) nature of how this formula interacts inside us, with the world, and with God. But it gets the important

---

[32] Carl R. Trueman, *The Rise and Triumph of the Modern Self: Cultural Amnesia, Expressive Individualism, and the Road to Sexual Revolution* (Wheaton, IL: Crossway), 2020.

pieces on the table. These are the universal, anthropological parts of the whole. We use mediators to get to the feeling state we desire in the midst of a dialectal life.

Why is this significant to lay out? Because the sum of your basic, collective spiritual intelligence falls into this simple rubric. The rubric elucidates the nature of your spiritual intelligence, which is defined by Wiseman and Watts as "an adaptive intelligence which enables people to develop their values, vision, and capacity for meaning."

To have an adaptive spiritual intelligence, it's important to see this operating system inside us. Resiliency is found in this understanding, between the tension of the polarizing dialectic and the recognition that there is a drive to emotional satisfaction. Identifying healthy and unhealthy mediators (the conditions of purpose, belonging, and values-based routines), is critical to the outcome of your ultimate desire. Therefore, it certainly follows how spiritual intelligence is essential to guide and provide wisdom to this end (figure 3).

Spiritual Resiliency

To find your best path to your ideal future self, your best path on your worst day, and the best path for your every day, you can be navigationally equipped with a spiritual compass and warrior code on your PRT Meaning Map. What are you navigating? You are navigating through or around the IDEAS, the external negative factors, the three internal negative factors (INFs), and how you apply your spiritual intelligence to the psychological effects of entropy and, most importantly, boundaries to your identity.

Spiritual resiliency utilizes the God-given resource of your spirit, activating the spiritual docking station, as Dr. Lisa Miller calls it. Spiritual resiliency is not a mental act of grit. It's using your spirit to help you find your best path. It's the act of prayer, meditation, or other transcendental practices to connect to God. This transcendental reaching during a significant time of difficulty, or even a peaceful time of thankfulness has tremendous evidence-based benefits. Most importantly, a spiritually resilient person knows that they are never truly alone.

Look at your PRT Meaning Map. Under Spiritual Intelligence, notice there are seven spaces to write in your top values and virtues. Remember: your life is always in draft. Whether you are proactively leaning forward into your horizon of hope or reacting to the entropic events of life, these seven spaces are provided for you to focus on your here and now.

This is where individual resiliency emerges. Ask yourself these questions:

- What do I spiritually need to believe now?
- What polarizing tensions am I experiencing?
- What is irritating my spiritual, psychological, or role identity?
- What projected (long distance) challenges are ahead, or what present (blocking) struggles do I need to react to?
- What spiritual virtues (attitudes) do I need to practice in this moment?
- What spiritual behaviors or practices do I need to live out now?
- Most importantly, what do I need to believe about my identity?

From the Judeo-Christian faith, you would want to assess yourself against the Fruit of the Spirit (Galatians 5:22-23), the Beatitudes (Matthew 5:2-12), or perhaps the Four Cardinal Virtues, (Prudence, Justice, Courage, Temperance). Do you need more faith? Do you need to practice love? Do you need to display patience? Do you need to discover more joy? What values and virtues are important to you now?

These are your values (beliefs) and virtues (attitudes and behaviors) that you are committing to in this moment on your horizon. Fill in your seven spaces under Spiritual Intelligence. If you are not reading this from a Christian perspective, there may be other spiritual values and virtues familiar to you that could fit your situation. You can also find a list of universal virtues to explore on the Trekk Unlimited website.

> Notice how these values and virtues can be connected to your values-based routines and belonging in life. How might you think of virtues in relation to values-based routines? What virtues motivate you to do them? Feel free to begin to write things down on your PRT Meaning Map. My current 7 under Spiritual Intelligence is Love, Prudence, Grit, Discernment, Joy, Loyalty, and Gentleness. This is what I'm focusing on now in my present conditions.

Your individual resiliency based on your spiritual intelligence is critical when you notice an encounter with a meaning gap. You come into contact with a situation that seriously challenges your identity. "Who am I?" All of a sudden, you are stuck, or your ideal future self feels so far away.

It can spin us into a negative self-identity. Negative scripts begin to roll out. We can feel biologically, physically depleted.

Spiritual intelligence adapts to this cycle with your values and virtues. It begins to reverse the negative script and realigns with your true spiritual identity and what you believe. You apply your beliefs on your PRT Meaning Map as a mediator for your life. It's your spiritual compass as you look out into your horizon of hope.

One time an officer struggling with alcohol addiction came to me. He felt helpless. His stated values didn't align with his daily actions. He wanted to quit alcohol. It was doing harm to himself and his family. I helped him recognize that alcohol was lying to him. It was not his friend. In fact, it was his enemy. It was destroying him. He went from feeling confused and helpless to being very angry. He got a hold of the courage inside himself to fight and determined that alcohol wasn't going to defeat him. I explained the PRT Meaning Map. He never returned to my office because he was able to use his spiritual intelligence and adapt to the ideal future self that he desired. He changed his values-based routine. He understood more completely that this was a moral and spiritual issue. This is spiritual intelligence related to resiliency.

Three Internal Negative Factors

As you already understand, our life is a dialectic. We live by codes, standards, laws, policies, customs and courtesies, weekly date nights with our spouse, and so forth. We often fail these moral codes or internally imposed standards. We *violate* standards—all the time. What do you do about it? Did you get caught? Do you hide? Do you admit? Do you just drive on? How do you feel about it? How you respond with your spiritual intelligence has a direct impact on your ability to be individually resilient, or resilient within your conditions of life. See figure 2.

The three internal negative factors are (1) violation, (2) guilt, and (3) shame. We violate, and we experience guilt and shame. If we do not adequately deal with the three INFs, we'll attempt to bury them or project a facade. That doesn't work. It always comes out somewhere else, like skeletons from a closet.

Remember: all of us have mediators. Mediators come from what is meaningful to us. The mediator is our religion. Mediators give us the feeling state we desire. Within your spiritual intelligence is a spiritual compass and warrior code. This is part of your conscience, which ought to be mediating your feeling state. Since our life is dialectal, we can converse with the mediator religion to get the priority feeling state we desire.

This is important when it comes to the three INFs. You need to be forgiven, reconciled, and free from guilt and shame. It will destroy you if you do not figure this out. You will not be able to reach your ideal future self nor find your best path on your worst day. I am concerned that our culture has vastly lost the spiritual compass and replaced it with Jack Sparrow's. Keep your spiritual compass recalibrating to true north.

5

Positive Self-Identity:
From Liquid to Solid

Scrolling through my Instagram feed, I ran across this Jocko Willink video quote. If you don't know him, he's a former Navy SEAL and motivational trainer. In the video, he was looking at you from a dark, subdued video frame, with mysterious, thrillerlike music playing in the background. He talked in very short, choppy sentences with his gruntlike, guttural voice. "Three questions. One, who are you? Two, who do you want to be? Three, how are you going to get there?" That was the end of the video.

That is what we all want. We want a plan or a map to get there, to close the gap. You are getting closer to it with your PRT Meaning Map.

> Orient yourself to positive self-identity (figure 6).

If you've already established your core spiritual identity, then it's easier to build out from there.

I want to say that the words *positive self-identity* are a little awkward. Right? It's like self-esteem. What is self-esteem? Psychology today says self-esteem really doesn't exist. Nevertheless, how you see yourself, your identity, whether negative or positive, is a fact. With two certifications in trauma therapy, I'm convinced by the effects of the use of eye movement desensitization reprocessing (EMDR), both personally and professionally. It facilitates change to have a PSI. Understanding trauma and therapy has caused me to conclude that this is a very important word.[33]

Ideal Future Self

As you know, I've extensively used the term *ideal future self,* and now you will get a chance to define it for yourself. Look at Ideal Future Self under Positive Self-Identity (Figure 6) on your PRT Meaning Map. You have already done the work for your purpose in life and belonging in life, and you've begun to think about your values-based routines.

Now including the above information, who do you want to be in one to five years? If you reflect all the way to your finish line, there is a Latin term, *memento mori*, which means remember you must die. Many people meditate on their future death to gain a present existential awareness of who they need to be. This is the beginning of a unified-focused resiliency. This is looking out to your horizon of hope, imagining the person you want to become. Think about who you want to be, what you want to do, who you want to do it with. Hold that image, but don't write it down just yet.

---

[33] Francine Shapiro, *Eye Movement Desensitization and Reprocessing: Basic Principles, Protocols, and Procedures,* 2nd ed. (New York, NY: Guilford Press, 2001).

Worst Future Self

Now who is the person whom you absolutely dread to become? When you think of all your worst proclivities and where they lead you, what does that person look like? Who is that person? Why do you not want to become that person? There's an old phrase that says, "You are you own worst enemy." What part of you is your own worst enemy? In Sun Tzu's *The Art of War*, this quote is instructive: "If you know your enemy and yourself, you need not fear the result of a hundred battles. If you know yourself but not the enemy, for every victory gained you will also suffer defeat. If you know neither the enemy nor yourself, you will succumb in every battle."

Think of your resiliency conditions: purpose, belonging, values-based routines. What are the threats to your ideal future self that can show up in your worst future self?

- Technology addiction
- Isolation and loneliness
- Illicit sex or porn addiction
- Substance abuse (food, drugs, alcohol, nicotine)
- Financial mismanagement
- Time (limitations or distractions)
- Unhealthy relationships
- Nihilism (hopelessness)
- Poor mental health
- Misappropriating identity
- Laziness
- Your ideal self (too much)
- Incoherent life (disorganized)

On your PRT Meaning Map, write out your worst future self. Be rigorously honest. From a Christian perspective you may want to consider the Works of the Flesh listed in Galatians

5:19-20, or the Seven Deadly Sins, (Pride, Greed, Wrath, Envy, Lust, Gluttony, and Sloth).

Now after writing out a profile of your worst future self, write down a vision of your ideal future self. Some language that you may want to include is the exact opposite of your worst future self. What positive virtues do you want to live out instead? How will people know you are moving toward this person in your character development?

Spiritual Compass (Highest Good)

Your spiritual compass, or highest good, is the morals, ethics, and religious or spiritual beliefs that you hold. Historically, there is a Latin term that brings this into focus: *Summon Bonum*. This means highest good. What are the highest good moral codes that you want to hold yourself to? On this line of your PRT Meaning Map, start writing the sentence "I will ...." A general example could look something like this, "I will wholeheartedly live for God. I will prioritize my family over competitive desires. I will not let pride and financial mismanagement interfere with my Ideal Future Self." Write as much as you desire. On the flip-slide of your Pathfinder Resiliency Tool, you have more space to write this out.

This is a declarative statement intending to influence your best path to your ideal future self and mitigate the worst path to your worst future self. This provides a unified-focused resiliency. Take your time to write in your moral warrior code. Commit to what you are going to do and what you are not going to do. Remember: what are you going to do to reconcile violations? Who or what is going to help you mediate failure?

Best Path on Your Worst Day

This is the reason why I wrote *Resilience Unlimited: How to Always Find Your Best Path*. All of us are going to have a worst day, most likely more than one, right? We are all going to experience the five IDEAS, the three INFs, and physical and psychological entropy. When you are at your wit's end and you need a best friend or two, a circle of trust, or a tribe, who are you going to call? Where are you going to go? What are you going to do, pathfinder? (If you are struggling with suicide right now and don't have any friends, call the national suicide hotline at 988.) Write the names of your best friends here. Now tell them that when you are having your worst day, you are going to reach out to them. Write out your plan now.

Rearview Mirror Exercise
Enhancing Your Positive Self-Identity

We are all toggling through our roles based on our various life settings: family, work, church, friendships, gym, hobbies, and so forth. Sometimes in those situations, we are subconsciously triggered by another's behaviors toward or around us. We emotionally unravel, and it's hard to pull it back together. Our identity is affected by brokenness from our past, and we might be suffering in the present.

I have permission to share a counseling session from a former elite special operations soldier who will remain nameless. When he walked into my office, he appeared to have it all together. Professionally, he had all the elite badges on his uniform to prove that he had been there and done that. He was in his mid- to late thirties, successful, handsome, super physically fit, incredibly intelligent, and married to a beautiful woman, and they had two young children together. Yet, he was struggling with a serious problem about his identity. He didn't know that was the issue.

He was in the presence of a group when a chaplain was talking, and he began to unravel. He had unfinished business to attend.

He shared with me that after numerous post-deployment debriefings with special operations psychologists, though he would initially talk about the gruesomeness of his combat experience, he would always return to his childhood traumatic experiences. He ultimately never fully processed it until his visit with me.

We were able to bracket the most difficult part of his childhood past: the event. Then I was able to facilitate for him how he saw himself (negative self-identity) in that moment. With tears rolling down this warrior's cheeks, he held up his wrist and showed me his watch. "Do you see this watch, Chaplain? This is a $37,000 watch. I wear this because I feel worthless inside." Looking at himself from that past event made this incredible hero feel worthless. He was carrying the burden of a negative self-identity.

Within one hour of EMDR therapy, he no longer had that negative belief about himself. He faced it, traced it, and replaced it with a positive self-identity that was already present within himself. I just facilitated an opportunity for him to psychologically re-sort himself where he was emotionally wounded as a child. His problem was that he couldn't get past the NSI blockage.

The Exercise

This is not therapy, but here is a spiritual exercise to enhance your PSI. It's an opportunity to spiritually process with God something from your past. If you are struggling with an NSI, such as "I'm not good enough" or "I'm unlovable" or "I'm stupid" or "I'm a failure," this is something that you can take to prayer and use with a journal to integrate into a more resilient PSI.

You can face it, trace it, and replace it. I also recommend a good therapist if you need one.

1. Who was I before this negative event? What positive qualities am I missing since it happened?
2. Who was I during this event? What was happening to me? How was I reacting positively and negatively?
3. Who am I now? How have I changed? Positively or negatively?
4. What does the loving voice of God (or my spiritual understanding) say to me?
5. Who do I want to be in the future?

Now take the best of the before, during, and now. Engage with God, your Mediator, and make a resolution to leave the worst (three INFs) in the past and bring the best to your future. Write this out as best as possible into a coherent new narrative. Update any Rear View Mirror events as you find it necessary.

6

The Horizon of Hope:
Your Future

In Suzanne Collins's book series and adapted movies *The Hunger Games,* President Snow is quoted as saying, "Hope. It is the only thing stronger than fear. A little hope is effective. A lot of hope is dangerous." The deepened, developed, diversified conditions (purpose, belonging, values-based routines) of our life mean we are going to have a dangerous amount of hope—unstoppable, resilient hope. How do we arrive at this?

When I reflect about the phenomenological aspects of looking into a horizon of hope, I can't think of any purer words than Catholic philosopher Charles Taylor's introduction to *A Secular Age.* He writes,

> Our highest aspirations and our life energies are somehow lined up, reinforcing each other, instead of producing psychic gridlock. This is the kind of experience which Schiller tried to understand with his notion of "play."
>
> These experiences, and others again which can't be all enumerated here, help us to situate a place of fullness, to which we orient ourselves

morally or spiritually. They can orient us because they offer some sense of what they are of: the presence of God, or the voice of nature, or the force which flows through everything or the alignment in us of desire and the drive to form.[34]

The horizon of hope is the result of all the six other meaning-making markers harmonizing together. It is the final output of the seventh marker. We need hopeful lives. Hope keeps us resilient. If our conditions are in tune through spiritual intelligence, meaning in life is present in us. If we have meaning in life, we feel a positive self-identity. When we have a PSI, we are hopeful about our future. As Taylor says, our life energies are somehow lined up, and we are without psychic gridlock. Life is like play. We're not experiencing too much entropy. This is incredibly idealistic, but somehow, we can't stop searching for this. We deeply desire it, and are cautioned to hold it lightly. So enjoy your life among what is good, true, and beautiful.

The Most Important Question in Life: Who am I?*

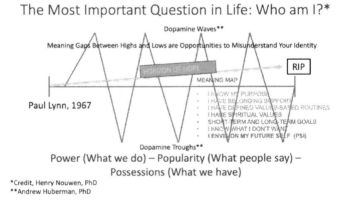

Figure 12

[34] Charles Taylor, *A Secular Age* (Cambridge, MA: Belknap Press of Harvard University, 2007), 6.

7

Authenticity for
Everyday Resiliency

One of the most grueling and rewarding experiences I had in the Army was attending the 82nd Airborne Division Pre-Ranger School in a remote location of Fort Bragg (now Fort Liberty), North Carolina. At the time, the course was a seventeen-day gut check. To pass the school and get a slot for the Fort Benning (now Fort Moore), Georgia, U.S. Army Ranger School, you had to be proficient in land navigation.

It started at midnight, and you needed to complete the course by six in the morning. That meant no sleep at all. You were already operating on about three hours of sleep from the night before. Setting out for this challenge you were equipped with these tools: map, compass, pencil, headlamp with a red light so as not to be visible, and army gear. It was thrilling.

The Pathfinder Resiliency Tool is like this. You are plotting a course. You now have a map, a clarified spiritual compass and warrior code. You are now more aware of the external and internal terrains of your life. To get from one point to the other, you have to, in navigational terms, shoot an azimuth. That's the line you draw on your map from where you are to the place you want to go. Then work your plan to that desired destination.

> Take out your PRT Meaning Map. When you look at the top, you see Horizon of Hope and Daily Azimuth Check. Ask yourself, "Am I going in the direction that I desire? Or am I being sidetracked by the spiritual enemies of my worst future self?"

This is a check-in with yourself! As a pathfinder in a constantly changing world, while looking at the horizon and your map, are there any physical, emotional, or spiritual obstacles preventing you from achieving your ideal future self? What impacts from the five ENFs (IDEAS) or three INFs are hindering you from achieving your goals? If you don't keep your eyes on the horizon and your PRT Meaning Map, you're likely to fall into mission drift. Because your life is always in draft, it's important to continuously coordinate with the ideal future self on your horizon of hope.

Real-time resiliency is dependent on staying on track with yourself and making course adjustments. The daily azimuth check is a discipline to see how authentically you are living toward your unified-focused resiliency. A definition of *authenticity* comes from neuropsychologist Theo Tsaousides: "Authenticity is acting according to one's true self and behaving congruently with values, beliefs, motives, and personality disposition."[35]

How are you authentically managing the conditions of your life? What resources (spiritual, physical, emotional, social, financial) do you need to keep you on track? You now have a PRT Meaning Map, which incorporates a spiritual compass, and a horizon of hope to do this.

---

[35] Theo Tsaousides, "What It Really Means to Be Authentic: In the End There Is Only One Answer," *Psychology Today.* Updated August 10, 2023, https://www.psychologytoday.com/gb/blog/smashing-the-brainblocks/202211/what-it-really-means-to-be-authentic.

A Tool for Spiritual Discipline

The Pathfinder Resiliency Tool Meaning Map is a spiritual solution in a time of meaninglessness and character fragility. This tool can accompany your Bible, journal, or other spiritual methods that can be a part of your values-based routines. Use the PRT Meaning Map in your personal quiet time. Carry it with you. It is a contemplative tool that can help you identify your ideal future self, best path on your worst day, and best path for your every day. It is my goal to have a future Resilience Unlimited—Pathfinder Resiliency Tool phone app. You can check yourself every day, update your map in real time, spiritually dial in to what you need to reflect about yourself and others, and act out your values and virtues. Your PRT will help you stay current with your circle of trust.

In conclusion, resiliency in the Resilience Unlimited—Pathfinder Resiliency Tool, as a mechanism, equips you with the possibilities to always find your best path. This is accomplished by foremost answering these three questions: 1) who am I spiritually? 2) who am I within the boundaries of social roles? 3) who am I within my psychological identity? The seminal answer comes from knowing what the voice of God has told you. It is your spiritual identity that provides the greatest resource of resilience. Writing this out on your Map gives you observable content for you to regularly reflect on and with others. Your PRT Meaning Map trains you to close the meaning gap, avoiding negative scripts by deepening, developing, and diversifying your conditions for possibilities. Finally, authentically living out your identity with your spiritual intelligence will equip you with the possibilities to always find your best path.

Postscript: Resilience Unlimited for Suicide Prevention

Since 2005 until my retirement, I have been providing resiliency and suicide prevention training for the US Army. I have been certified in the Applied Suicide Intervention Skills Training (ASIST) and the Ask, Care, Escort (ACE) model. The latter involves critical skills for chaplains and leaders to know and use as the final gatekeeper in suicide prevention. This isn't enough.

The Seven Meaning-Making Marker model is a true resiliency training model in the preventive sense. It's easy to train using figure 3 in less than one hour. Materials on this can be found in the Resilience Unlimited Field Manual, ordered through the Trekk Unlimited website: www.trekkunlimited.com.

Our world, not just our military, needs this now. As we say in the Army, "We need to get left of the boom." The Resilience Unlimited—Pathfinder Resiliency Tool can educationally equip all people with the knowledge that it's normal to have suicidal ideas if you are experiencing catastrophic meaning loss. It might be normal, but it's not healthy. Again, it's not healthy, but in clustered meaning loss it will seem normal to have a negative self-identity and possible suicidal ideations. Catastrophic meaning loss with the clustering of the categories from the five IDEAS is absolutely devastating. It can disintegrate our identities into meaninglessness.

What does this look like?

- When one's Purpose-in-Life no longer exists or threatened
- When one's significant Belonging-in-Life no longer exists or threatened
- When Roles (*both* Purpose and Belonging) no longer exists or threatened
- When one's Values-Based Routines no longer exists or threatened
- When one's Spiritual Intelligence is ill-equipped for catastrophic meaning loss
- Then, one's Psychological Identity begins to collapse or shatter

Gatekeeper training is critically necessary, but building the ark before the inevitable flood is too. We need this preventive, conditions-based, unified-focused resiliency handheld tool. Our world needs to know that resiliency is not just about mental health. It's fundamentally spiritual health.

Resilience Unlimited, as a preventative mechanism, trains the client to build resilient conditions, live a unified-focused life, and quickly closes the spiritual and psychological gap created by the five IDEAS. Resilience Unlimited helps you answer the question asked of us every day, "Who am I?" It brings your spiritual identity, and spiritual intelligence into critical focus and aligns the role and psychological identity in its proper place.

Check out these reports sent to me about the *Resilience Unlimited* training. These are a few samples. "My biggest take-away was that spiritual resilience is so much more than just religious beliefs and it confirmed my self-worth and identity." Another said, "I didn't think of, or know my personal mission statement until today."

Here's a real text message from a soldier to a chaplain that was sent to me by another chaplain using this tool. The soldier was seriously struggling before he started this training. Afterward, his life began to get traction and have hope. I changed the content to reflect anonymity.

Soldier: "Chaplain, when can we please meet again so I can learn more about resiliency? This material is really helping me!"

Chaplain: "Meet me at my office on Monday at 0900. Looking forward to see you again."

Soldier: "I can't wait!"

Now, let's do this on mass scale for our culture experiencing meaninglessness and fragility.

Appendix I

Organization Pledge for a
Pathfinder Resiliency Group

1. I pledge to join the Pathfinder Resiliency Group (PRG) to build personal, conditions-based, unified-focused resiliency in my life and the life of other pathfinders. This is the purpose of the PRG.

2. I will meet fellow pathfinders several times a month at dates and times determined by the PRG.

3. I will support other pathfinders in reaching their ideal future self through a defined positive self-identity.

4. I will respect the values of each pathfinder. I recognize that everyone has different values from me. If I am unable to do this, then I will respectfully remove myself from the PRG.

5. I will listen to others as well as process with the PRG the values and virtues of other pathfinders to live out a horizon of hope.

6. I pledge to have each pathfinder's back, especially to help them find their best path on their worst day.

Appendix 2

Suggested Structure for
Pathfinder Resiliency Group

- Forty-five to sixty minutes
- Three to eight pathfinders
- Facilitator leading a small group
- Welcome by the pathfinder facilitator
- Pathfinder facilitator reminding the PRG about the pledge of respect
- Keeping the PRG time on target
- Encouraging participation (in first person) and cautioning about oversharing
- Each taking a turn in giving a two- to five-minute update on (1) how one sees oneself in the present situation; (2) how one sees the ideal future self, looking into a horizon of hope; (3) how one is applying the spiritual compass to conditions; (4) where one needs to improve the conditions and apply spiritual intelligence to the positive self-identity
- After everyone's check-in, facilitate group feedback from one another for improvement, where each pathfinder solidifies solutions by integrating short-term and long-term plans as appropriate
- Closing (next date and time) and optional moment of silence or prayer

Appendix 3

Resilience Unlimited Questionnaire
(Digital version at www.trekkunlimited.com)

Likert Scale, 1–5
1: Strongly Disagree
2: Disagree
3: Neither Agree nor Disagree
4: Agree
5: Strongly Agree

- Take the Resilience Unlimited Questionnaire before reading the book and filling in your PRT Meaning Map.
- Use your PRT Meaning Map for one month daily.
- Retake the questionnaire and see what has changed.
- Give special focus to a growth area for multiple questions answered, especially items that score 1) Strongly Disagree, 2) Disagree
- Give consideration to 3) Neither Agree nor Disagree.
- Note: it is your input conditions (Purpose, Belonging, Values-Based Routines, and Spiritual Intelligence) that result in your output conditions (Meaning, Positive Self-Identity, and Hope)

Four Purpose Questions

1. I am confident about my future goals in life.
2. I feel satisfied about the trajectory of the important things I want to do in life.
3. In the things I want to do in life, I *do not* often feel stuck.
4. What I realistically want to do in life seems obtainable.

Four Belonging Questions

1. I have close bonds with family and friends.
2. I have a strong sense of belonging to a community.
3. I *am not* worried about being alone or isolated.
4. In a hard time, there are people I can count on to help me.

Four Values-Based Routine Questions

1. I am good at practicing habits, disciplines, and regular traditions that help my life.
2. My values shape my habits so I can be successful in my goals.
3. I prioritize my habits to get the best possible results.
4. I am good at prioritizing important relationships to keep them strong.

Four Meaning Questions

1. Both my work and relationships give me a strong sense of meaning in life.
2. My work gives me a strong sense of meaning in life.
3. My relationships and community give me a strong sense of meaning in life.
4. My job is *not* the most important part of my life.

Four Spiritual Intelligence Questions

1. I have a defined set of beliefs and values that give my life a sense of purpose and direct me on how I handle relationships.
2. My spirituality informs and guides my relationships and future.
3. I have certain ways of practicing my spirituality.
4. I am confident that my morals, ethics, and spiritual values will shape a positive future.

Five Identity Questions

1. I have a balanced perspective about what other people think about me.
2. When I think of my future, I am *not worried* about the person I want to become.
3. I am able to manage both thoughts of unduly negative or unduly positive self-identity.
4. I feel good about myself because of strong relationships, and I'm attaining my goals in life.
5. I practice good boundaries in my role relationships that give me confidence and hope.

Four Hope Questions

1. When I look into my future, I am very hopeful.
2. I feel hopeful when I think about my purpose in life.
3. I feel hopeful when I think about all my significant relationships.
4. I feel hopeful because I am disciplined in life, which helps me reach my goals.

Appendix 4

A Pluralistic Analysis of Resilience Unlimited from the Turkish Brigade

A pluralistic example that includes all Seven Meaning-Making Markers comes from the Korean War. The Turkish Brigade soldiers who were taken as prisoners had a 100 percent survival rate. In the same operated prisons of war, the Americans had a 40 percent loss of life.[36] What was the difference? The Turks had greater military discipline, which I call values-based routines. They were more closely knit together in their belonging in life, and they had a strong spiritual compass from their Islamic religion.

It was well known that the ethnically homogenous Turks followed a very strict code of military discipline. They had a great sense of national pride. Their reputation of caring for one another was indomitable. They were unshakeable together as they withstood enemy brutality. And their religious practices within the camp gave them a metaphysical resource, spiritual resiliency. It was these conditions that provided their purpose in life to survive, which gave them meaning in life. They were oxygen rich in purpose, belonging, values-based routines, and spiritual connection, which kept their sense of self intact to be

---

[36] Patricial B. Sutker et al., "Cognitive Deficits and Psychopathology among Former Prisoners of War and Combat Veterans of the Korean Conflict," *American Journal of Psychiatry* 148, no. 1. (January 1991): 67.

resilient (see *FM 7-22*, paragraph 10 citation under Integrated Model of Resiliency).

It is the position of this author that other religions and meaning-making systems of thought such as a military code of conduct can provide frameworks of resiliency. When the Seven Meaning-Making Markers have robust presence within an individual, along with a cohort of similar minds and spirits, the possibilities to win have increased.

Appendix 5

All-Star Endorsements

Chaplain (Major) Ret. Paul Lynn's impactful contributions to the development of the Spiritual Readiness Initiative (SRI) stand out as a pioneering effort during my tenure as the Chief of Chaplains. In the face of the pressing challenges surrounding suicide and the imperative for readiness and a resilient spirit, Paul's innovative approach has proven instrumental. I am convinced that a deepened sense of spirituality is critical to navigating these crises, offering individuals the profound sense of meaning that is pivotal to overcoming adversities. It brings me immense joy to witness the ongoing progression of his work in this book. The enduring impact of this work underscores the transformative role of spirituality and to forge resilient paths forward.

Chaplain (Major General), USA, Ret. Thomas L. Solhjem
25th Chief of Chaplains, United States Army

What are you using to fill "The Gap?" Paul gives you the answer to one of the most important questions you'll ever ask! The Gap is the space between who you really are and who you wish you were. Read this book if you're looking for timeless, battle-tested advice on eliminating "the gap" in your life."

Pastor Jeff Struecker, Ph.D.
Black Hawk Down, U.S. Army Ranger Hall of Fame
Silver Star Recipient
Retired U.S. Army Chaplain
Host of Unbeatable Podcast

Thanks to the research of Angela Duckworth and others, the topic of grit or resiliency is being recognized as a crucial factor in living a fulfilled and successful life. In *Resilience Unlimited*, Chaplain Paul Lynn has produced a worthy addition to this literature. This book has been forged in the context of the incredibly difficult work of a U.S. Airborne Chaplain with boots on the ground (literally) with his soldiers.

Suicide is an issue in the U.S. military, and the principles Chaplain Lynn puts forth here have saved real lives in extraordinarily difficult situations. Among the most important principles he discusses is a commitment to begin with the guided identification of a person's spiritual, role, and narrative identities and from there to construct purpose and values statements, belonging activities, and values-based routines that will provide directional guidance even when there are setbacks in life. As Chaplain Lynn writes, these principles will help you find your best path even on your worst day. I encourage you to not only read *Resilience Unlimited* but also invest the time working through the embedded exercises. Everyone can benefit from strengthening their resiliency!

Gregory J. Miller, Ph.D.
President
Malone University
Canton, OH USA

Paul Lynn, in his groundbreaking book about resilience, brings out the dynamic interplay of underrecognized factors, leading us to our ultimate center of gravity, an identity found in God. It's from this vantage point, that a person can be resilient in their role identities and psychological identities, how you see yourself. With this sense of resiliency, a horizon of hope opens up so that you can find a God-sized vision. In this book, he shows us how to do it and provides a much-needed tool to always keep resilient conditions in the present.

Mark Batterson
NYT Best Selling Author, The Circle Maker
Lead Pastor, National Community Church

I can't believe how timely this book is. Coming out of a pandemic so many professional and elite athletes are in crisis of identity. Paul gives us a playbook of how to help navigate our self-worth to become better versions of ourselves. Identity is a resounding issue when it comes to athletes as they are driven for success in sport and in social media. *Resilience Unlimited* will give you the tools needed to carve out a plan for a more fulfilling life, not only for those you influence but also for you. I have already started to implement these tools with Olympic athletes and even myself.

Asif Shaikh
Four-time Olympic Chaplain
Life Coach to Elite Athletes

Chaplain Lynn provides us with a robust tool to deeply understand who and how we are so we can intentionally decide who we'd like to be. Well-researched and holistic in its approach, this resource is a living template for personal change. The author does not impose upon us another anxiety-producing "method," but offers us a path to resilient growth by exploring our own purpose, values, identity, and spirituality. I strongly encourage all to walk this path.

Chaplain (Colonel), USA, Ret. Steven J. Moser
LMFT-S
Former Director of the Family Life Center, Fort Hood, TX

In the realm of organizational success, competent leadership is paramount for strategically maneuvering against competition and achieving victory. Chaplain (Major) Ret. Paul Lynn has not only recognized this necessity but has also crafted an effective program, Pathfinder: Finding Your Best Path on Your Worst Day. His latest offering, *Resilience Unlimited* goes even further, providing a comprehensive guide that extends beyond that previous work. By adhering to the principles and tools outlined in this book, one can embed resiliency principles at the core of your organization or personal life, ensuring relevance both now and in the future.

Having served alongside Paul during combat operations in Afghanistan, I witnessed firsthand his deep understanding and embodiment of God's calling. In the face of violent situations, he didn't just "talk the talk" but authentically "walked the walk." I wholeheartedly recommend *Resilience Unlimited* to those aspiring to set and achieve high goals, pushing themselves to the limits of personal growth, family dynamics, and career success.

Chaplain (COL) USA, Ret. Terry L. McBride
Former United States Army Special Operations Command Chaplain

Printed in the United States
by Baker & Taylor Publisher Services